MARY R

A Play in Three Acts

by

J. M. BARRIE

SAMUEL FRENCH LIMITED

LONDON

SAMUEL FRENCH. LTD.
26 SOUTHAMPTON STREET, STRAND, LONDON, W.C.2

SAMUEL FRENCH, INC.
25 WEST 45TH STREET, NEW YORK, U.S.A.
7623 SUNSET BOULEVARD, HOLLYWOOD 46, CAL.

SAMUEL FRENCH (CANADA), LTD.
480 UNIVERSITY AVENUE TORONTO

SAMUEL FRENCH (AUSTRALIA) PTY., LTD.
159 FORBES STREET, SYDNEY

MADE AND PRINTED IN GREAT BRITAIN BY
BUTLER AND TANNER LTD., FROME AND LONDON
MADE IN ENGLAND

MARY ROSE

A play, in three acts, by Sir James Barrie. Produced April 22nd, 1920, at The Haymarket Theatre, London. Last performance (the 398th), February 26th, 1921.

MRS. OTERY	*Miss Jean Cadell.*
MR. MORLAND	*Mr. Norman Forbes.*
MRS. MORLAND	*Miss Mary Jerrold.*
MR. AMY	*Mr. Arthur Whitby.*
MARY ROSE	*Miss Fay Compton.*
HARRY	
SIMON BLAKE	*} Mr. Robert Loraine.*
CAMERON	*Mr. Ernest Thesiger.*

The action of the play, which covers a period of over thirty years, passes between a small manor house in Sussex and an island in the Outer Hebrides.

SYNOPSIS OF SCENES

ACT I
The Home of the Morlands.
SCENE 1.—As it is to-day—1919.
SCENE 2.—As it used to be—1889.

ACT II
The Island—1894.

ACT III
The Home of the Morlands.
SCENE 1.—As it used to be—1917.
SCENE 2.—As it is to-day—1919.

MARY ROSE

ACT I

SCENE 1

*The SCENE—which is to undergo an odd change early in the act—is
at first an unfurnished room in a small manor house in England
in 1919.*

The time is the present—a chilly November afternoon.

*It is an upstairs room in an empty house which has been to sell
for some time and is in a dreary dilapidated condition—damp and
neglect everywhere doing their fell work. A melancholy dis-
honoured sort of room—all the more so because there is a suggestion
of its having once been bright and comfortable, the happy home of
gentlefolks though not of great people. The owner, indeed, had
been " The Squire," but a very small one. The room is panelled
and should show the marks of inattention and some discoloration.
It is a small room, the smaller the better, and low in the ceiling.
For reasons connected with the last act, there must be a good deal
of space between the back wall of the room and the back of the stage.
(See the Ground Plan at the end of the book.)*

*On R. up stage is the entrance to the room. The fireplace, at
present unlit, is in the middle of the L. wall. There is a window
of the french kind down to the floor in the back wall with unseen
steps from it to the ground. In the back wall is also a door
opening on to a short passage with another door at the end of it.
This further door will be invisible to any part of the audience.
The visible door is the important one in the play. The window,
which is also important, should be sufficiently small to seem a real
window and not the enormous thing common on the stage. It has
no curtains nor blinds, but some rough sacking is nailed over it,
covering only part of it, so that some light still struggles in. Thus
the room is not actually dark, but it is far from light. The only
furniture is a worn old easy chair L.C., large but in a state of
decay, and two rough wooden packing cases. A dreary scene that
strikes a chill.*

*As the CURTAIN rises the door R. is opened by MRS. OTERY. Then
someone is heard clumping up the stairs and HARRY enters.
MRS. OTERY is a caretaker, of something under forty, a dull
woman who has lost the sense of enjoyment long ago. She seems
a natural part of this forlorn abode. She has probably shown
many possible purchasers over the house, and she has the true
caretaker's indifference as to whether you mean to buy or not.
But at times, as we shall see, there is something strange about her*

5

—as if she knew that the house had an ill-name, and was anxious to conceal it, and was herself a little frightened, like one who has been sometimes scared by the presence that haunts the house. This gives her at times a furtive look. HARRY, who is about twenty-six, is an Australian soldier—a private, and is in the uniform that of late years has become so familiar to our streets. He has the Australian tang in his voice, manners and movements. He is a rough fellow from sheep farms and the bush, sinewy, physically wiry, with the " peeled " eye of the man with the axe whose chief life struggle has been to fell trees without letting trees fall on him. He is not a " sympathetic " character in this scene though he is likeable rather than otherwise. MRS. OTERY is showing him the house which he has evidently known in other days, but though he is interested he is far from sentimental, and looks about him with a tolerant grin.

Enter MRS. OTERY. She is very conscious of the door up L.C. and shudders as she looks at it.

MRS. OTERY. Are you coming up ?
HARRY (*off*). What's your hurry, my cabbage ? There's lots of time.

(He enters and goes L.)

MRS. OTERY (*after he has surveyed the room*). When the house was furnished this was the drawing-room.
HARRY (*looking around and shaking his head*). Not it, no, no— never ! This wasn't the drawing-room, my cabbage—at least not in my time.
MRS. OTERY. I've just been here three years and I never saw the house furnished, but I was told to say this was the drawing-room. And I would thank you not to call me your cabbage.
HARRY. No offence. (*Humorously.*) It's a French expression, and many a happy moment have I given the mademoiselles by calling them cabbages. But the drawing-room ! I was a little shaver when I was here last. But the drawing-room—we called it the Big Room, it wasn't a little box like this.
MRS. OTERY. This is the biggest room in the house.
HARRY. Snakes, whether it's the room or not, it's clammy cold—something shiversome about it. (*He shivers, and moves a little down L.C.*)

(For the first time she gives him a sharp glance.)

Many a hut I've shivered in in the Bush in Australia, and thought of the big room here and the warmth of it. And this is the best it can do for the Prodigal when he comes back expecting to find that calf done to a turn ! We live and learn, missis. (*He moves to the hearth and turns.*)
MRS. OTERY. We live, at any rate.

HARRY (*moving a little towards her*). Well said, my cabbage.

MRS. OTERY. Thank you, my rhododendron.

HARRY (*with a cheerful grin*). I like your spirit. (*He goes to her.*) You and me would get on dandy if I had time to amuse myself with your womanly weaknesses. (*Moving towards the window.*) I tell you what—I can make sure whether this was the drawing-room. If it was, there's an apple-tree outside there, with one of its branches scraping on the window.

(*She has followed. He turns to her.*)

I ought to know, for it was out at that window down that apple-tree to the ground that I slided one dark night when I was a twelve-year-old, ran away from home, the naughty blue-eyed angel that I was, and set off to make my fortune on the blasted ocean. The fortune, my lady friend, is still dodging round the corner—but the apple-tree should be there to give me the glad eye.

(*He turns to the window and pulls down the sacking, which lets more light into the room, but does not brighten it as the afternoon is a dreary one. There is no tree, but we see a small railing, which is the beginning of the steps down. MRS. OTERY steps to R. of the window.*)

(*Referring to pulling down the sacking.*) Avec apologies. You see ! No tree—no drawing-room.

MRS. OTERY. I've heard tell there was once a tree there—and you can see the root if you look down. (*She goes to the door.*)

(HARRY *rubs the frame with his sleeve and looks down without opening the window.*)

HARRY. Yes, I see it in the long grass, and a bit of the seat that used to be round it. (*He turns from the window.*) It's the drawing-room right enough, Harry, my boy ! There were blue curtains to that window, and I used to hide behind them and pounce out on Robinson Crusoe. (*He crosses* L.C.) There was a sofa just *here*, where I had my first lessons in swimming. You're a fortunate woman, my petite, to be here drinking in these moving memories. There used to be a peacock, too. Now what the hell could a peacock be doing in this room ?

MRS. OTERY (*who has moved a little down* R.C.). I've been told there was an old fire-screen with peacocks worked on it. I dare say that's your peacock.

HARRY. Gone—even my peacock ! And I would have sworn I used to pull the feathers out of his tail ! The clock stood there. My old man used to wind that clock up every night. Every night ; and I mind his rage when he found out at last it was an eight-day clock. The padre had to reprove him for swearing. Padre ? What's the English for Padre ? Damme ! I'm forgetting my own language. Oh, yes, parson. The two of them were always quarrelling about prints they collected. I can see them sitting there at a table quarrelling and my old lady, bless her dear old heart, in the sofa by the fire there knitting and smiling at their bickerings and getting them to make it up. Is the parson in the land of the living still? I can see him clear—a little thin man with a hard sharp face.

Mrs. Otery. The parson here is a very old man, but he's stoutish with white whiskers. (*She turns a little up* c.)

Harry. Whiskers? (*Strolling to the packing case* R.C.) I can't think he had whiskers. *Had* he whiskers? Stop a bit—I believe it's his wife I'm thinking about! (*Above the packing case.*) I doubt I don't give satisfaction as a sentimental character. Is there any objection, your ladyship, to smoking in the drawing-room? (*He takes a cake of tobacco and a clasp knife from his pocket.*)

Mrs. Otery (*ungraciously*). Smoke if you want.

(*She turns to stare at the door up* L.C. *He cuts tobacco for a few moments then turns to her.*)

Harry. What are you staring at that door for?

Mrs. Otery (*turning, startled*). Nothing! That's a fearsome-looking knife!

Harry. Useful in warfare, old toucher. It's not a knife—it's a visiting card. Like this, with comps. (*He casts it at one of the packing cases, and it sticks, quivering in the wood. He leaves it there and lights his pipe.*)

Mrs. Otery (*coming down a pace* c.). Were you an officer?

Harry (*crossing below her to* L.C.). Not me—don't insult me, woman! I *began* by being an officer. (*He turns to her, confidentially.*) See here—after I'm gone, give me twenty-four hours' start, and then you can tell the neighbourhood that you had a visit from the man who won the war.

(*NOTE.—Neither of them sits in this scene, till* Harry *sits at the end of it.*)

Mrs. Otery. You're playing with me.

Harry. It's my *manly* weakness. You're so *ir*resistible.

Mrs. Otery (*grunting disapproval of him*). Do you want to see the other rooms? (*She moves down* R.C.)

Harry (*burlesquely*). I was fondly hoping you would ask me that. I would like to see the room just above here where we used to store the apples. A low dark place it was but the apples were good. My father—Simon was his name—once caught me in the apple room and—but these be family secrets.

Mrs. Otery. Come, then. (*She moves* R.)

Harry (*to up* c.). Wait a jiff. What does this door you were staring at open on? (*He looks at the door up* L.C.)

MRS. OTERY (*who wants to get him away from that door*). Nothing—just a cupboard.

HARRY (*turning on her*). Oh! (*Fixing her.*) Who's playing with *me* now?

MRS. OTERY (*curtly*). I don't know what you mean. Come this way. (*She makes to move* R., *but checks as he speaks again.*)

HARRY (*not budging*). I'm a patient cuss. I'll explain what I mean. That door—it's coming back to me—it leads into a little dark passage——

MRS. OTERY. That's all.

HARRY. That can't be all. Who ever heard of a passage wandering about by itself in a respectable house? It leads—yes!—to a single room, and the door of the room faces this way. Doesn't it?

(*She does not answer. A pause.*)

You're a regular old gossip. We'll soon see. (*He turns and opens the door and we see the other door beyond.*) There's a memory for you. But what the hell made you want to deceive me?

MRS. OTERY. It's of no consequence. That's the cupboard door, at the end of the passage.

HARRY. Cupboard? (*Reflecting, in the doorway.*) It's no cupboard—it's a room with two stone windows—and wooden rafters.

MRS. OTERY. It's the oldest part of the house.

HARRY (*coming down a pace*). It comes back to me that I used to sleep there.

MRS. OTERY. That may be. If you'll come—— (*She is always wanting him to follow her.*)

HARRY. And you pretend it's a cupboard! I'm curious to see that room first. (*He turns up towards it.*)

MRS. OTERY (*thin-lipped and determined*). You can't go in there.

HARRY (*bluntly, turning to her*). Your reason? (*He comes down* C. *after closing the door.*)

MRS. OTERY (*after a slight pause*). It's locked. (*She takes a pace towards him.*) I tell you it's just an empty room. Nothing in it but dust and decay. No human being has crossed the threshold of it for months.

HARRY. There must be a key.

MRS. OTERY (*after hesitation*). It's lost.

HARRY (*coming down* L.C.). Curious your anxiety to stop me, seeing you knew I would find the door locked. (*Turning to face her.*) Was it just an admirer's kindness to save me from taking half a dozen steps? (*He moves a pace up* L.C.)

MRS. OTERY (*in a little outburst of appeal*). Leave that room alone.

HARRY (*he checks and turns to study her*). You're all shivering.

MRS. OTERY (*controlling herself*). I'm not.

HARRY (*looking towards the fire*). I suppose it's because this room is so clay cold.

MRS. OTERY (*falling into the trap*). That's it !

HARRY (*sharply, turning on her*). So you *are* shivering !

(*She does not answer, but turns to the door* R.)

Can I put a light to those bits of sticks ?

MRS. OTERY (*checking at* R.C.). If you like. My orders are to have fires once a week.

(HARRY *lights the sticks in the fireplace, which burn up easily, but will be exhausted in a few minutes. She closes the door and comes* C.)

I believe I'm just wasting my time. *You* can't have the money to take a house like this.

HARRY (*watching the fire*). Not me ! It's not my billet. It was just curiosity brought me here. I'm for Austraty again. (*Suddenly turning round and going to her.*) What's wrong with this house ? (*He gets more serious from this point.*)

MRS. OTERY (*on her guard*). There's nothing wrong with it.

HARRY. Then how is it going so cheap ?

MRS. OTERY. It's in bad repair.

HARRY. How has it stood empty so long ?

MRS. OTERY. It's so far from a town.

(*The light now fades slowly to the end of the scene.*)

HARRY. What made the last tenant leave in such a hurry ?

MRS. OTERY (*wetting her lips, turning away*). You've heard that, have you ? Gossiping down at the White Horse——

HARRY. I've heard some other things as well. I've heard they had to get a caretaker from a distance, because no woman here about would live alone in this house.

MRS. OTERY (*moving down* R.C., *facing down stage*). A parcel o' cowards !

HARRY (*quicker, his voice raised*). I've heard that that caretaker was bold and buxom when she came, and that now she's a scared woman.

MRS. OTERY (*huskily*). I'm not.

HARRY (*as before, moving to above and* L. *of her*). I've heard she's been known to run out into the fields and stay there trembling all night.

(*She does not answer. He is cunning, and crosses* L., *speaking more casually.*)

Of course, I see it couldn't have been you. Just foolish stories that gather about an old house.

MRS. OTERY (*relieved*). That's all.

HARRY (*swinging round suddenly, to trick her, looking at the door up* L.C.). What's that ?

(MRS. OTERY *screams, and turns to face up* L.C., *the pent-up fear in her getting the mastery for the moment.*)

(*Turning to face her.*) I got you that time !

(MRS. OTERY *turns away* R.C.)

What was it you expected to see ?

(*There is no answer.*)

Is it a ghost ? They say it's a ghost. What sort of a wally-walloo is it gives this house an ill-name ?

MRS. OTERY (*harshly*). Use as brave words as you like when you've gone, but I advise you, my lad, to be cautious while you're here. (*More matter-of-fact.*) There's no use showing you the rest of the house. If you want to be stepping I have my work to do. (*She moves* R. *towards the door.*)

HARRY. My train's not for an hour yet, and we've got on so nicely, I wonder if you would give me a mug of tea. Not a cup, we drink it by the mugful where I hail from.

MRS. OTERY (*ungraciously*). I see no reason—but I have no objection.

HARRY (*bows*). Since you're so pressing I accept.

MRS. OTERY. Come down to the kitchen. (*She goes up* R.)

HARRY (*crossing* L.). No, no, I'm sure the Prodigal got his tea the first day in the drawing-room——

MRS. OTERY. I see what you're up to. You're meaning to go into that room. I wouldn't if I was you.

HARRY. Maybe if you were me you would. (*Going up* C.)

MRS. OTERY (*taking a pace up stage*). Unless I have your promise——

(*She checks as* HARRY *rounds on her*)

HARRY (*harshly*). What the blazes has your ghost to do with me ? (*He pauses, then speaks softly.*) It's a woman, isn't it ?

(*Her silence is a sort of assent. He is serious.*)

What has—brought her back—to this house ?

(*There is no answer. She turns away* R.C. *He becomes sarcastic, moving down* L.C.)

See here, I'll sit in this chair—saying my prayers in case she tries to get me. (*He sits* L.) It's an even thing that she may be some relative of mine and if so the least she can do is to introduce herself and tell me for what uncanny object she haunts **my** ancestral home. By jugs! There's a lot of ghosts might gather round this chair now if they knew that Harry my lad had come back. Well, I'm ready for them—let 'em all come! (*He slaps the chair-arms and addresses the chair.*) You're a mouldy damp, old dear. (*To* MRS. OTERY.) It's not the ghost's chair by any mishap, is it?

(MRS. OTERY *makes no answer. Her face betrays her.*)

You needn't look so scared, woman, she doesn't walk till midnight, does she? That's their hour, as I've always heard.

MRS. OTERY. You're a brave lad, you're thinking. (*Going towards the door, looking at the knife still sticking in the wood.*) I wouldn't leave that knife lying about, sonny.

HARRY. Oh, come, give the old girl her chance. She is old, I suppose?

MRS. OTERY. I've warned you. I'll not be more than ten minutes.

HARRY. She can't do much in ten minutes.

(MRS. OTERY *fixes him with her eyes, and then goes out* R. *It is beginning to get dark. He sits in the chair, mending the fire; while he is doing so the door up* L.C. *opens about two feet silently, and remains so. As* HARRY *then crosses* R. *this door slowly closes. All this takes place in a few seconds, in which* HARRY *is mending the fire. He suddenly jerks round, starting to his feet at the same time. What is to be conveyed is that he is convinced there is someone in the middle of the stage. He is so sure this is the place that for a moment he looks nowhere else. Enough time—three seconds—elapses to have made it possible for an unseen person to have gone from the middle of the stage to the door up* L.C. *He has not seen the door open, and turns round just too late to see it close. He has been genuinely startled, and now strides up* L.C. *to the door and throws it open, calling out:*)

Is anyone there?

(*He brushes his eyes, like one who has been dazed. He leaves the door open, goes down to his knife to get it. He takes the knife but throws it again into the box top, implying that there it is for the ghost if she can get it. He sits down again in the chair* L. *and looks round sharply, once at* C. *of the stage and then at the inner room. All this, though elaborately described, is quite brief—a very few seconds only. As he sits in the chair there is no suggestion that he is falling asleep. The stage darkens until all is blotted out. The fire is the last light to be extinguished.*
Start the music when all light is out.)

CURTAIN.

Scene 2

Scene.—*The room as it used to be in 1889.*

When the Curtain *is up, a pool of light slowly reveals the table* R.C., *followed by all other lighting slowly to full up.*

With the briefest pause possible we again see the same room, but it is now the cheerful cosy room of thirty years earlier—as warm and homely as it has hitherto been cold and neglected. We see some of the things Harry *has referred to : the curtains, the clock, the tapestry with peacocks on it, etc. There are a number of coloured prints on the wall, for* Mr. Morland *in an amateur way is a collector. It is a sunny forenoon in May, the window is open, and the apple tree in full blossom is much in evidence— one of its branches has even got a little way into the room.*

There are three people in the room, all a little over forty years of age. They are the Squire and his wife, i.e., Mr. *and* Mrs. , Morland, *and the local clergyman.* Mr. Morland *is only a little squire of very moderate means. For instance, though we never see servants in the house it may be said he had not more than three, and they are all women. He is the type of man who passes his life pleasantly and not unprofitably in being a J.P. and will discuss for days or months the advisability of putting a new roof on a tenant's cowshed. His wife is a very delightful little lady, a mixture of sunshine and shrewd sense. Her preserves, ciders, roses, lavender, etc., are undoubtedly the best in the district, and she has a joke that has kept her merry through all her married life, viz. her husband. She adores him, however, and they are a very lovable couple.* Mr. Amy *is a dear creature of a clergyman, quite unlike* Mr. Morland *in appearance, and they are close friends except when they have momentary quarrels about prints, for print collecting is their hobby, and each likes to show the other his latest purchase and gloat over it until the other says jealously that it is worthless when they nearly come to blows. A very common scene between them is such a one as now follows. The two men are sitting by a table, looking at some prints, unframed, which* Mr. Morland *is showing to his guest.* Mrs. Morland *is outside the talk, she is sitting by the fire, placidly knitting, occasionally smiling to herself over their words.* Morland *has a print hanging in his hand which he passes across to* Amy.)

Amy (*taking the print and examining it*). Very interesting. A nice little lot ; I must say, James, you have the real collector's flair for engravings.

Morland (*a trifle complacently, sitting back*). Oh, well, I'm keen, you know, and when I run up to London I can't resist going a bust—in my small way. I picked these up quite cheap.

Amy. Did you really ! You have the real flair.

Morland. Oh, I don't know.

AMY. Yes, you have, James. You got them at Holman's in Dean Street, didn't you ? Yes, I know you did. I saw them there. I wanted them, too, but they told me you had already got the refusal.

MORLAND. Sorry to have been too quick for you, George, but it's my way to nip in. You have a very nice collection yourself.

AMY. I haven't got your flair, James.

MORLAND. I admit I don't miss much !

AMY. No. (*Complacently.*) You missed something yesterday at Holman's though.

MORLAND. How do you mean ?

AMY. You didn't examine the little lot lying beneath this lot.

MORLAND. I turned them over—just a few odds and ends of no account.

AMY (*beaming over his own cleverness*). All except one, James.

MORLAND (*in an agony, glancing at MR. AMY*). Something good ?

AMY (*with wicked meekness*). Just a little crayon drawing by Gainsborough.

MORLAND. What ! (*Sitting erect.*) You've got it ?

AMY. I've got it. I'm a poor man, but I thought fifteen shillings wasn't too much for a Gainsborough.

MORLAND (*gasping*). Fifteen shillings ! (*He rises.*) Is it signed ?

AMY. No, it isn't signed.

MORLAND (*significantly*). Ah ! (*He sits, very relieved.*)

AMY (*sharply*). What do you precisely mean by that " Ah ! ", James ? You can't be so ignorant as to think it was usual to sign them. If it had been signed, could I have got it for fifteen shillings ? You are always speaking about your flair—I suppose I can have a little flair sometimes, too.

MORLAND. I'm not always speaking about my flair, and I don't believe it *is* a Gainsborough !

(MRS. MORLAND *coughs, as a sign to her husband to be more polite. He understands and obeys.*)

After all, perhaps it is, George.

AMY (*with dignity*). Please don't get so hot, James. If I had thought you would grudge me my little find—which *you* missed —I wouldn't have brought it to show you.

MORLAND. You've brought it !

(AMY *takes up a drawing which is between cardboards from under his chair and displays it.*)

So that's it ! (*Looking at it.*)

AMY. This is it ! There ! I have the luck this time ! I hope you will have it next. (*Facing MORLAND, smiling.*)

(MORLAND *rises, takes the print to the window and examines it with foreboolings.*)

Well ?

MORLAND (*with a sigh of relief, returning to above the table*). Interesting, George—quite. But definitely not a Gainsborough.

AMY (*firmly*). I say definitely a Gainsborough.

MORLAND. Definitely not a Gainsborough. (*He puts the print down on the table.*) I should say the work of a clever amateur.

(*They are getting pugnacious.* MR. AMY *rises and moves to* R. *of* MR. MORLAND.)

AMY.   Look at the drawing of the cart and the figure beside it.

MORLAND.   Weak and laboured. (*Pointing.*) Look at that horse !

AMY.   Gainsborough did some very funny horses.

MORLAND.   Granted. But he never placed them badly. (*Tapping the print.*) That horse destroys the whole balance of the composition.

AMY.   James, I had no idea you had such a small nature !

MORLAND.   You're making yourself ridiculous.

(MRS. MORLAND *coughs.* MR. MORLAND *moves down to the chair* L. *of the table.*)

My dear old fellow, no one would have been more pleased than myself if you had picked up a Gainsborough—but this ! (*He sits.*) Besides, look at the paper !

AMY.   What's wrong with the paper, Mr. Morland ?

MORLAND.   It's machine-made.

(AMY *sits, above the table.*)

Gainsborough was in his grave years before that paper was made.

(AMY *examines the paper in a frenzy and is evidently convinced against his will, while* MORLAND *is horridly pleased.*)

AMY.   Oh ! (*He puts the print between the cards, rather savagely.*)

(MRS. MORLAND *coughs.*)

MORLAND.   Mind you, I think it's a very pretty thing.

AMY.   Not you !

MORLAND.   Don't get into a tantrum about it, George.

AMY (*rising*). I'm not in a tantrum—and I would be obliged if you wouldn't " George " me. (*With huffy dignity and nearly crying.*)

(MRS. MORLAND *puts down her knitting.*)

(*Tucking the picture under his arm.*) Smile on, Mr. Morland, I congratulate you on your triumph. You have hurt an old friend to the quick. Bravo! Bravo! (*He goes to* MRS. MORLAND *and shakes hands.*) I thank you, Mrs. Morland, for a very pleasant visit. Good morning. Good morning.

(*He crosses towards* R., *with offended dignity.* MRS. MORLAND'S *attitude throughout has been that of one accustomed to these scenes, smiling occasionally, but going on calmly knitting. She now rises to play her familiar part, having already carefully put down her knitting.*)

MRS. MORLAND. I shall see you into your coat, George.

AMY (*near the door* R.). I thank you, Mrs. Morland. I require no one to see me into my coat.

(*He exits, and she trots blandly after him.* MORLAND, *left alone, begins to be a bit ashamed of himself and puts his prints in a drawer of the bureau* R.)

MORLAND (*as he crosses* R.). Silly fellow! Silly fellow—a Gainsborough! (*He crosses up* R. *to the window and looks out over the garden.*)

(MRS. MORLAND *returns with* AMY *who is wearing his coat, leading him like a child.*)

MRS. MORLAND. Now which of you is going to say it first? (*She coughs and moves to the* R. *end of the settee.*).

(*The two men speak simultaneously.*)

AMY ⌠ (*Above and to* R. *of the table*). James, I am heartily
　　 ⎱ ashamed of myself.
MORLAND ⎧ (*Moving up to above and* L. *of the table*). George, I
　　　　 ⎩ apologize.

AMY. I quite see that it isn't a Gainsborough.

MORLAND. After all, it's certainly in the Gainsborough school.

AMY. I want to say, James, that you do really have a flair.

MORLAND. Not so much as you, George.

AMY. Far more, far more, I have no flair.

MORLAND. Yes, you have.

AMY. No, I have not. (*He stamps his foot.*)

(MRS. MORLAND *coughs.* AMY *extends his hand.*)

James!

MORLAND. George!

(*They shake hands sheepishly. Then they look at* MRS. MORLAND, *who has sat down with a newspaper which conceals her face.* AMY *shakes his fist at her, smiles and exits* R. MRS. MORLAND *puts down the paper.*)

(*Crossing to* L.C. *and taking the paper from the settee.*) He's a good chap, George, but he has no flair. He might as well order his bargains, as he calls them, by telephone.

MRS. MORLAND (*resuming her work*). By what ?

MORLAND (*believing in what he is telling her*). Telephone, it's called. (*He crosses to the fireplace and turns.*) It's a new invention. There's an article about it in this paper. Very wonderful ! The writer says that in a few years' time people sitting here, for instance, will be able to talk to people in London !

MRS. MORLAND (*placidly*). Nonsense, James.

MORLAND (*his back to the fire, reading the paper*). And yet, there's no denying as he says that there are more things in heaven and earth than are dreamt of in our philosophy.

(*There is a little silence between them.*)

MRS. MORLAND (*becoming grave*). You and I know that to be true, James.

MORLAND. Eh ? (*He lowers the paper and they exchange looks.*) Oh, that ? Oh, well, that's all dead and done with long ago.

MRS. MORLAND. Yes. But sometimes when I look at Mary Rose—so happy——

MORLAND. *She* will never know anything about it.

MRS. MORLAND. No, indeed. But some day she will fall in love——

MORLAND. That infant ! Fanny, is it wise to look for trouble before it comes ?

MRS. MORLAND (*after a slight pause*). James, she can't marry without——

(MORLAND *looks at her.*)

We agreed.

MORLAND. I'll keep my word. (*He sits on her* L.) I'll tell the man everything.

MRS. MORLAND. Poor Mary Rose !

MORLAND. Now then, none of that. Where is she now ?

MRS. MORLAND. Down at the boat-house with Simon, I think.

MORLAND. That's all right. Let her play about with Simon and the like. It may make a tomboy of her, but it will keep young men out of her head.

MRS. MORLAND (*she wonders at his obtuseness*). You still think of Simon as a boy ?

MORLAND. Bless the woman ! He's only a midshipman.

MRS. MORLAND. A sub-lieutenant now.

MORLAND. Same thing. Why, I still tip him. At least, I did a year ago. And he liked it ! " Thanks no end, you are a trump," he said, and then slipped behind the screen to see how much it was ! (*He chuckles.*)

B

MRS. MORLAND. He is a very delightful creature—but he isn't a boy any more. ✓

MORLAND. It's horrible of you to put such ideas into my head. I'll go down to the boat-house at once. (*Rising and moving to* R. *of the settee.*) If this new invention with wires was in working order, Fanny, I could send him packing without rising from my seat. First, we are to ring a bell. (*He pulls at an imaginary bell.*) Then speak into a sort of cup : " Hullo, boat-house, is my little Mary Rose there ? " (*He makes the cup out of the newspaper.*)

(*To the surprise of both there is an answer from* MARY ROSE *unseen.*)

MARY ROSE (*in a quaking voice*). I'm here, Daddy !

(*They look round.*)

MORLAND. Where are you, Mary Rose ?

MARY ROSE. I am in the apple tree !

(*They look at each other and smile.* MRS. MORLAND *is going to rise, but* MORLAND *checks her, and resumes his telephonic manner.*)

MORLAND. What are you doing in the apple tree ?

MARY ROSE. I'm hiding.

MORLAND (*still as into telephone*). From Simon ?

MARY ROSE. No. I'm not sure whom I'm hiding from. From myself, I think. (*Squeaking.*) Daddy, I'm frightened.

(MRS. MORLAND *half rises but is again checked by* MORLAND. *She sits again.*)

MORLAND. What has frightened you ? Simon ?

MARY ROSE. Yes—partly.

MORLAND. Who else ?

MARY ROSE (*speaking again*). I am most afraid of you.

MORLAND. Of *me* ? Afraid of me ? (*He exchanges a look with* MRS. MORLAND.) Odd ! (*He goes to the* R. *window.*)

MRS. MORLAND. You absurd pair ! (*Raising her voice a little.*) Mary Rose, come in at once—and let this be the last time you enter a drawing-room by climbing up a tree.

(MARY ROSE *enters, apparently hanging on to one branch and walking lightly along another. She is a very pretty girl of about nineteen, capable of the wildest gaiety and fun, a gleeful child, over-full of happiness and little aware of the future that lies before her. She is really extremely impulsive, capable of many emotions at present hidden beneath the surface. As we see her for the first time she is a girlish mixture of joy and fright, over the terrific event that has been happening at the boat-house.*)

MARY ROSE. Mother ! (*She runs across to her mother, hides*

in her bosom, looks up, then hides her face again at thoughts of the awfulness of her news.

(MRS. MORLAND *is by no means as dense about what is to be told her as her husband is.* MORLAND *moves down to above and* L. *of the table.*)

MRS. MORLAND. You don't mean that anything has really frightened you, Mary Rose ?

MARY ROSE (*looking up*). I'm not sure. Hold me tight, Mother. (*She clings again to* MRS. MORLAND.)

MRS. MORLAND. Darling, has Simon been distressing you ?

MARY ROSE (*almost vindictively*). Yes, he has. It's all Simon's fault.

MORLAND (*taking a pace to* C.). I'll lick him !

MARY ROSE. Yes !

MORLAND. But you said you were even frightened of me.

MARY ROSE. You are the only one !

MORLAND. No one was ever frightened of me before. Is this some new game ? Where is Simon ?

MARY ROSE (*goes to* MORLAND). He is at the foot of the tree. He is not coming up by the tree. He wants to come in by the door. (*Appealingly.*) That shows how important it is.

MORLAND. What is ?

MARY ROSE (*trying to be explanatory*). You see, it's like this. Simon's leave is up to-morrow, and he—(*shakily*) wants to see you, Daddy, before he goes.

MORLAND (*chuckling*). I'm sure he does ! And I know why. I told you, Fanny. Mary Rose, do you see my purse lying about ? (*He looks round.*)

MARY ROSE (*faintly*). Your purse, Dad ?

MORLAND (*crossing to the fireplace*). You, you gosling. There is a fiver in it, and *that's* what Master Simon wants to see me about. (*He sits below the fireplace.*)

MARY ROSE (*moving to the* R. *end of the settee, giving her mother a despairing look*). Mummy ! (*She again buries her head on her mother's bosom.*)

MRS. MORLAND (*she has guessed*). Oh, James ! Dearest, tell me what Simon has been saying to you.

(MARY ROSE *is shy and buries her face.*)

Then whisper it, my love.

(MARY ROSE *whispers.*)

Yes, I thought it was that.

MARY ROSE (*childishly*). You won't let Daddy be angry with me, will you ?

MRS. MORLAND. James, you may as well be told bluntly ; it isn't your fiver that Simon wants—it's your daughter !

MORLAND (*with a shout, rising*). What ?

(MARY ROSE *runs* L. *and clings to him.*)

MARY ROSE (*coaxingly*). You'll scold him, won't you, Dad ?

MORLAND (*almost speechless*). By—by—by—by all that's horrible I'll do more than scold him ! The puppy, I'll—I'll——

(MRS. MORLAND *rises.*)

MARY ROSE (*appealing*). Not *more* than scold him, Daddy—not *more*. I couldn't bear it if it was *more* !

MORLAND (*rather shaky now, but kind*). You are not in love with Simon, are you ? (*Holding her at arm's length.*)

(*Her face gleams—she nods.*)

What in particular do you see in him ?

MARY ROSE (*in a long-drawn-out ecstasy*). Oh-h-h-h ! (*She runs as if ashamed to* MRS. MORLAND—*then, quaintly.*) Daddy—Mummy—— (*She runs to* MORLAND, *then to her mother, who has sat again.*) I'm so awfully sorry that this has occurred. (*She screws up her face and weeps openly and hysterically, sitting* L. *of* MRS. MORLAND.)

MRS. MORLAND. My own, my pet. (*Soothing her.*) But he is only a boy, Mary Rose—just a very delightful boy !

MARY ROSE (*her eyes shining and her manner almost solemn*). Oh, Mother, that is the wonderful, wonderful thing. He *was* just a boy—I *quite* understand that—till eleven o'clock to-day. But you'll scarcely know him now, Mother.

MRS. MORLAND. Darling, he breakfasted with us. I think we shall know him still.

MARY ROSE. He is quite different from breakfast time. He has grown so grave, so manly, so—so *protective* ! He thinks of everything now, even of freeholds and leaseholds—and gravel soil—and the hire system—and (*she breaks down again*)—and hot and cold——

MORLAND (*firing up a little*). He's got as far as that, has he ? Does he propose that this marriage should take place to-morrow ?

MARY ROSE (*eagerly, to soften the blow*). Oh, no, not for quite a long time. At *earliest*, not till his next leave.

MRS. MORLAND. Mary Rose ! ·

MARY ROSE. He is waiting down there, Mummy. (*Rising.*) May I bring him in ?

MRS. MORLAND. Of course, dearest.

(MARY ROSE *crosses towards* R.)

MORLAND. Don't come with him, though.

MARY ROSE (*checking at* R.C.). Oh! You know how shy Simon is.

MORLAND (*testily, turning to the fire*). I do *not*!

MRS. MORLAND (*rising and touching his arm*). Your father and I must have a talk with him alone, dear.

MORLAND. Yes, that's always done.

MARY ROSE. Is it? Oh, well—he so wants to do the right thing, Mother.

MRS. MORLAND (*to* L.C.). I'm sure he does.

MARY ROSE. Do you mind my going upstairs into the apple room, (*she looks at the ceiling*) and sometimes knocking on the floor? I think it would be a help to him to know I am so near by.

MRS. MORLAND. It would be a help to all of us, my sweet.

MARY ROSE. I won't be able to hear what you are saying, but *how* I shall imagine it! (*She crosses back* R. *to* MORLAND.) I love him so! You—you won't try to put him against me, Daddy?

MORLAND. I would do my best if I thought I had any chance! (*He kisses her.*)

(MARY ROSE *gives him a hug, and runs off through the windows and is heard clattering down the stairs. The clatter of* MARY ROSE *on the stairs is always noticeable. No other person does it.* MR. MORLAND *goes kindly to* MRS. MORLAND *whose eyes are wet.*)

Poor old mother!

(*They sit on the settee.*)

MRS. MORLAND. Poor old father! You know, James, there are times when——

(MARY ROSE *runs in with two parts of a fishing rod, which she quickly puts together and lays on the table.*)

MARY ROSE (*mysteriously*). There's a reason for this!

(*She runs out, through the windows.*)

MORLAND. Simon's fishing rod. What can they be up to?

(*Clattering is heard.*)

MRS. MORLAND. Some nonsense, James; what a pleasant sound in this house is Mary Rose clattering up and down the stairs and making more noise than all the rest of us put together.

MORLAND. How awful if we're to cease to hear it!

MRS. MORLAND. There couldn't be a nicer boy, James.

MORLAND. It got me on the quick when she said, "You won't try to put him against me, Daddy"—because that is just what I suppose I have got to do.

MRS. MORLAND. Yes, he must be told.

MORLAND (*suddenly*). Fan, let's keep it to ourselves.

MRS. MORLAND. It wouldn't be fair to him.

MORLAND (*rising and crossing to the fire*). No, it wouldn't. (*He turns to* MRS. MORLAND.) He'll be an ass if it bothers him.

MRS. MORLAND (*timid*). Yes.

MORLAND. He's coming! Oh, dear! I think I look my firmest in a stiff chair. (*He sits* L., *below the fireplace.*)

(SIMON *comes in at the door* R., *a manly fellow of twenty-three, in flannels. Though played by the same actor, he should be very different from* HARRY. *He is as smart as* HARRY *is slouching ; he is essentially a jolly young fellow, while* HARRY *was hard, bitter and rather morose ; his manner is frank and open, while* HARRY *was rather a cynic ; he has an educated voice, while* HARRY'S *had the tang of the Bush. He is fresh-complexioned, while* HARRY *was sallow. At present he is in a state of mingled exaltation and trepidation, and moves, by shy stages, to* C.)

SIMON (*in a sort of foolish hysteria*). Ha, ha, ha, ha, ha, ha, ha, ha !

MORLAND. You will need to say more than that, you know, Simon, to justify your conduct.

MRS. MORLAND. Oh, Simon, how could you ?

SIMON. It seems almost like stealing.

MORLAND. It *is* stealing.

SIMON. Ha, ha, ha—ha, ha, ha !

(*Here there is a knocking on the floor above which gives him courage.* MR. *and* MRS. MORLAND *smile but pretend not to hear it.*)

(*After a glance towards the ceiling.*) It's beastly hard on you, of course—but if you knew what Mary Rose is——!

MRS. MORLAND. We feel that even *we* know to some extent what Mary Rose is !

SIMON. Yes, rather ! (*Cleverly.*) And so you can see how it has come about. (*He feels he has scored.*) I would let myself be cut into little chips for her, I would almost like it ! (*Regretfully.*) Perhaps you have thought that in the past I was rather a larky sort ?

MORLAND. Well, rather breezy . . . (*Sarcastically.*) But we see an extraordinary change in you, Simon, since breakfast.

SIMON (*eagerly with a pace to* L.C.). Have you noticed that ? Mary Rose has noticed it, too. That's my inner man coming out. (*Carefully saying things to make a good impression.*) To some people marriage is a thing to be entered on lightly, but that is not my style. What I want is to give up larks, and all that, and insure my life and read the political articles.

(*More knocking above, which reminds him of something else.*)

Oh, yes! and I promise you it won't be like losing a daughter, but like gaining a son!

MRS. MORLAND. Did Mary Rose tell you to say that?

SIMON (*guiltily*). Well——

(*There is more knocking.*)

(*Crossing to below the* L. *end of the settee.*) Oh, another thing, I should consider it well worth being married to Mary Rose, just to have you, Mrs. Morland, for a mother-in-law!

MORLAND (*pleased*). Well said, Simon—I like you the better for that.

MRS. MORLAND. Did she tell you to say that also?

SIMON. Well——

(*More knocking.*)

At any rate, never shall I forget the respect and affection I owe to the parents of my beloved wife.

MORLAND (*testily*). She's not your wife yet, you know.

SIMON. But can she be, Mrs. Morland? Can she be?

MRS. MORLAND. That is as may be, Simon. It is only a possible engagement that we are discussing at present.

SIMON. Yes, of course. I used to be careless about money, but I have thought of a trick of writing the word "Economy" in the inside of my watch so that I'll see it every time I wind up. My people——

MORLAND. We like *them*, Simon.

(*More knocking from above.*)

SIMON (*crosses* C. *and looks up*). I don't know whether you've noticed a sound from up above?

MORLAND. I did think I heard something!

SIMON. That's Mary Rose!

MRS. MORLAND. No!

SIMON. Yes. She's doing that to help me. I promised to knock back as soon as I thought things were going well.

MRS. MORLAND. So that's what the fishing rod was for?

(*They are moved. He puts the fishing rod together and stands on a chair to knock on the ceiling.*)

SIMON. What do you say? May I?

MORLAND (*to* MRS. MORLAND, *wistfully, rising*). I think, my dear, he might?

(SIMON *is still on the chair* C.)

MRS. MORLAND (*braver*). No!

(*She rises and moves to* R.C. MORLAND *moves to below the settee.*)

There is a little thing, Simon, that Mary Rose's father and I feel we ought to tell you about her before—before you knock, my dear boy. It's not very important, I think, but it's something she doesn't know of herself, and it makes her a little different from other girls. (*She turns the chair* L. *of the table to face down stage.*)

SIMON (*getting off the chair, sharply*). I won't believe anything against Mary Rose.

MRS. MORLAND. We have nothing to tell you against her. (*Asking her husband to do his part.*) James! (*She sits* L. *of the table.*)

(SIMON *moves behind* MRS. MORLAND *to* L.C. MORLAND *stands below the* R. *end of the settee.*)

MORLAND. It is just something that happened, Simon. She couldn't help it. It hasn't troubled us in the least for years, but we always agreed that she mustn't be engaged before we told the man. (*He puts his hand on* SIMON'S *shoulder.*) We must have your promise before we tell you that you will keep it to yourself.

SIMON (*disturbed, but dogged*). I promise.

(MORLAND *drops his hand, and turns to the fireplace, as* SIMON *goes to* L. *of* MRS. MORLAND.)

MRS. MORLAND. You must never speak of it even to her.

SIMON. Not to Mary Rose ? I wish you would say quickly what it is.

MORLAND (*returning to below the* R. *end of the settee*). It can't be told quite in a word. It happened seven years ago, when Mary Rose was twelve. We were in a remote part of Scotland— in the Outer Hebrides.

SIMON. I once went ashore there from the " Gadfly "—very bleak and barren, rocks and rough grass—I never saw a tree. (*He sits on the* R. *arm of the settee.*)

MRS. MORLAND. It's mostly like that.

MORLAND. There's a whaling station. We went because I was fond of fishing. I haven't had the heart to fish since. But where we were there is an inland loch, and in it—a little island—a little island——

(*The mention of the island moves both* MR. *and* MRS. MORLAND *and he has difficulty in going on. A slight pause.*)

MRS. MORLAND. It is quite a small island, Simon— uninhabited——

MORLAND. No sheep even—I suppose there are only about six acres of it.

MRS. MORLAND. There are trees there—quite a number of them—a very uncommon thing in the Hebrides. Scotch firs and a few rowan trees—they have red berries, you know ! There seemed to us to be nothing very particular about the island— except perhaps that it is curiously complete in itself. There is a tiny pool in it that might be called a lake out of which a stream flows. It has hillocks and a glade—a sort of miniature land. (*Tremulously.*) That was all we noticed, though it became the most dreaded place in the world to us.

MORLAND (*because she is agitated*). I can tell him without your being here, Fanny.

MRS. MORLAND. I would rather stay, James.

MORLAND. I fished a great deal in that loch! The sea-trout were wonderful. I often rowed Mary Rose across to the island and left her there to sketch. I could see her from the boat most of the time, and we used to wave to each other. Then I would go back for her when I stopped fishing.

SIMON. Didn't you go with them, Mrs. Morland?

MRS. MORLAND. Not often, Simon. I was mostly at our little house, not far away in the village. We didn't know at the time that the natives had a superstition against landing on the island, and that the island was supposed to resent this. It had a Gaelic name which means " The Island that Likes to be Visited." Mary Rose knew nothing of this, and she was very fond of her island. She used to talk to it—call it her darling— things like that.

SIMON. Tell me what happened.

MORLAND (*sitting, at the* R. *end of the settee*). It was on what was to be our last day. I had landed her on this island as usual, and in the early evening I put up my rod while still in the boat and from there I could see her sitting on a stump of a tree that was her favourite seat, and she waved gaily to me and I to her. Then I rowed over to fetch her, with, of course, my back to her.

(*A pause.* SIMON *stands.*)

I had less than a hundred yards to go, but Simon, when I got across—she wasn't there!

(MR *and* MRS. MORLAND *are agitated.* SIMON *crosses to above the table.*)

SIMON. You seem so serious about it. She was hiding from you.

MRS. MORLAND. She wasn't on the island, Simon.

SIMON. But—but—oh, but——   (*He sits above the table.*)

MORLAND (*rising*). Don't you think I searched and searched? (*He moves to* L.C.)

MRS. MORLAND (*turning to* SIMON). All of us! No one in the village went to bed that night. It was then we learned how they feared the island.

MORLAND (*behind* MRS. MORLAND'S *chair*). The loch was dragged. There was nothing we didn't try—but she was gone.

SIMON (*rising, distressed*). I can't—there couldn't—but never mind that. (*To* R. *of the table.*) Tell me how you found her.

MRS. MORLAND. It was the thirtieth day after she disappeared —thirty days !

SIMON. Some boat——

MORLAND. There was no boat—but mine.

SIMON. Tell me.

MRS. MORLAND. The search had long been given up, but we couldn't come away.

MORLAND (*to above the table*). I was wandering one day along the shore of the loch—you can imagine in what state of mind. I stopped and stood looking across the water at the island—and Simon, I saw her sitting on the tree-trunk sketching !

MRS. MORLAND. Mary Rose !

(SIMON *sits* R. *of the table.*)

MORLAND. She waved to me and went on sketching. I—I waved back to her. (*Speaking a little more quickly.*) I got into the boat and rowed across just in the old way, except that I sat facing her, so that I could see her all the time. When I landed, the first thing she said to me was : " Why did you row in that funny way, Dad ? " (*Slowly, after a slight pause.*) Then I saw at once she didn't know that anything had happened.

SIMON (*rising*). Mr. Morland ! How could—somebody must —(*looking at* MRS. MORLAND)—where did she say she had been ?

MRS. MORLAND. She didn't know she had been anywhere, Simon.

MORLAND (*moving to* L.C.). She thought I had just come for her at the usual time.

SIMON. Thirty days ! You mean she had been on the island all that time ? (*He goes up to the windows and stares out.*)

MORLAND. We don't know. (*He drops down to below the settee.*)

MRS. MORLAND. James brought her back to me just the same merry unself-conscious girl, with no idea that she had been away from me for more than an hour or two.

SIMON (*turning from the windows*) But when you told her—— (*Moving to* L.C.)

MRS. MORLAND. We never told her ; she doesn't know now.

SIMON (R. *of the settee*). Surely you——

MRS. MORLAND (*turning in her chair to face him*). We had her back, Simon—that was the great thing. At first we thought to tell her after we got her home—and then, it was all so inexplicable, we were afraid to alarm her—to take the bloom off her. In the end we decided never to tell her.

SIMON. You told no one ?

MORLAND. Some friends and doctors in London.

SIMON. How did they explain it ?

MORLAND. They had no explanation for it, except that it never took place. You can think that too, if you like.

SIMON (*taking a pace towards* MORLAND). I don't know what to think. It has had no effect on her, at any rate.

MORLAND. None whatever, and you can guess how we used to watch.

MRS. MORLAND (*rising and moving a little towards* SIMON). Simon, I am very anxious to be honest with you. I have sometimes thought that our girl is curiously young for her age—as if—you know how just a touch of frost may stop the growth of a plant and yet leave it blooming—it has sometimes seemed to me as if a cold finger had once touched my Mary Rose.

SIMON. Mrs. Morland!

MRS. MORLAND. There's nothing in it.

SIMON. That's her youth, her innocence—which seems a holy thing to me.

MRS. MORLAND. And indeed it is! (*She moves down below, and* R. *of the table and turns.*)

SIMON (*crossing up* O.). If that's all——

MORLAND. Simon——

(SIMON *checks at* O.)

—We have sometimes thought that she had momentary glimpses back into that time, but before we could question her in a cautious way about them the gates had closed and she remembered nothing. You never heard her talking casually to some person who—who couldn't possibly be there?

SIMON. No.

MRS. MORLAND. Nor listening for a sound that wasn't there?

SIMON. A sound? Do you mean a sound from the island?

MRS. MORLAND. Yes, we think so. But she has long outgrown these fancies. (*She turns to the bureau and takes out some sketches, bringing them to* SIMON.) These are some sketches she made. You can take the book away and look at them at your leisure.

(SIMON *takes the book.* MORLAND *turns down to the fireplace.*)

SIMON. It's a little curious that she has never spoken to me of that holiday in the Hebrides. She tells me everything.

MRS. MORLAND (*below and* L. *of the table*). No, that isn't curious—it is just that the island has faded out of her memory. I should be troubled if she began to recall it. Well, Simon, we felt we had to tell you. (*Crossing to below the settee.*) That's all we know, I am sure it is all we shall ever know. (*Turning to* SIMON.) What are you going to do?

SIMON (*stoutly*). What do *you* think?

(*He gets on the chair above the table, knocks and gets answering knocks in return. The shadow has passed from his face and he is smiling happily again.* MORLAND *crosses* L.O.)

You heard ?   That means it's all right.   You'll see how she'll
come tearing down to us !

MRS. MORLAND (*rises and goes to him*).   You dear boy.   (*She
gives him a little hug.*)   And you'll see how I shall go tearing up
to her !

(*She goes off* R., SIMON *opening the door for her.*   MORLAND *moves
to* L.C.)

SIMON (*comes* C.).   I do love Mary Rose, sir.

MORLAND.   So do we, Simon.   I suppose that made us love
her a little more than other daughters are loved.   Well, it's dead
and done with, and it doesn't disturb me now at all—I hope you
won't let it disturb you.

SIMON.   Rather not.   (*He pushes the chair* L. *into the table.*)
I say, what *can* be the explanation ?

MORLAND.   I am sure you will think of a number of things,
but we have thought of them all before—and it's no good.   We
did wisely, didn't we, in not telling her ?

SIMON.   Oh, Lord, yes !   "The Island that Likes to be
Visited."   It's a rather sinister name, I think.   (*Boyishly.*)   I
say, let's forget all about it.   (*He looks at the ceiling.*)   I almost
wish her mother hadn't gone up to her.   It will make Mary Rose
longer in coming down.   (*He moves to above and* R. *of the table.*)

MORLAND (*with humorous solemnity*).   Fanny will think of
nicer things to say to her than you could think of, Simon.

SIMON (*down* R. *of the table*).   Yes, I know.   (*Then he sees he is
being chaffed.*)   You're chaffing me !

(MORLAND *moves to* L.C.)

(*He spars playfully at* MR. MORLAND.)   You see, sir, my leave is
up to-morrow.   .

(*A clatter of steps, and* MARY ROSE *comes rushing in.*)

Mary Rose !

(MARY ROSE *darts past him into her father's arms.*   SIMON *comes
to below the table.*)

MARY ROSE.   It isn't you I'm thinking of—it's Father !   It's
poor Father !   Oh, Simon, how could you ?   Isn't it hateful of
him, Daddy ?

MORLAND.   I should just say it is !   Are you crying ?

MARY ROSE.   Yes.

MORLAND.   Is your mother crying too ?

MARY ROSE (*squeaking*).   Yes.

MORLAND.   I see I'm going to have a beastly day.   (*He passes*
MARY ROSE *across to his* L. *and moves* R.)   If you two don't mind
very much being left alone, I think I'll go up and cry with your
mother in the apple room.   (*Turning at the door.*)   It's close and

dark and musty up there, and when we feel we can't stick it any longer I'll knock on the floor, Simon, as a sign that we are coming down.

(*On this light note he goes off* R. SIMON *opens the door.* MARY ROSE *and* SIMON *are shy of each other. They stand a yard apart.*)

SIMON. Mary Rose ! (*He moves up* L.C.)

MARY ROSE. Oh—Simon, you and me !

SIMON. You and me ! That's it—we are *us* now. (*In a whisper.*) Do you like it ?

MARY ROSE (*whispering*). It's so fearfully solemn.

SIMON. You are not frightened, are you ?

(*She nods.*)

Not at me ?

(*She shakes her head.*)

What at.

MARY ROSE. At *it*—being—married. (*Going to him, at* L.C.) Simon, after we are married you will sometimes let me run out and play, won't you ?

SIMON. Games ?

(*She nods.*)

Rather. Why, I'll go on playing rugger myself. Lots of married people play games.

MARY ROSE. I'm glad.

(*She leads him to the settee. They sit.*)

Simon, I want to ask you something. Do you love me ?

SIMON. Dearest . . . precious . . . sweetheart. . . . Which name do you like best ?

(*They are both solemn.*)

Which—darling, be brave and tell me.

MARY ROSE. I'm not sure. They are all very nice.

SIMON. I think just Mary Rose is the prettiest name of all. What do you think is the nicest name for a man ? If you would answer that, it would make such a difference to me.

MARY ROSE. I think there is one name almost nicer than Simon.

SIMON. What ?

MARY ROSE. It's Harry ! I don't know why it seems such a nice name to me. I have never known a Harry—but I should rather like if ever—— (*She hides her head on him.*)

SIMON. What are you thinking of, Mary Rose ?

MARY ROSE. Please don't ask me, Simon dear.

SIMON. I won't.

MARY ROSE (*looks at the ceiling*). I think we are selfish. Oughtn't we to ask those beloveds to come down ?

SIMON. Honest Injun, it isn't selfishness. You see, I have a ton of things to tell you. About how I put it to them, and how I remembered what you told me to say—and the way I got the soft side of them ! They have heard it all already, so it would really be selfish to bring them down.

MARY ROSE (*wondering*). I'm not so sure. It's mouldy there, and you can't stand straight up.

SIMON (*rising, to c. and turning*). I'll tell you what we'll do. We'll go back to the boat-house and then they can come down and be cosy here.

MARY ROSE (*rising, gleefully*). Let's ! We can stay till tea-time.

SIMON. It's fresh down there—put on a jacket.

MARY ROSE. Jacket—bother !

SIMON (*firmly*). My child—you are in my care now—I am responsible for you—I *order* you to put on a jacket.

MARY ROSE. Simon, you do say the loveliest things! I'll put it on at once. (*She crosses up* L.C., *and turns.*) Simon, I'll tell you an odd thing about me—I *may* be wrong, but I *think* I'll sometimes love you to kiss me, and then at other times it will be better not. (*She comes down to him* L.C.)

SIMON. All right. Tell me, what were you thinking as you sat up there, waiting ? Do tell me.

MARY ROSE (*whispering*). Holy things !

SIMON. About love ?

(*She nods.*)

MARY ROSE. We'll try to be good, won't we, Simon, please ?

SIMON. Rather. Honest Injun, we'll be nailers. Did you think of—our wedding day ?

MARY ROSE. A little.

SIMON. Only a little ?

MARY ROSE. But frightfully clearly.

(*He kisses her hand.*)

(*She sits on the* R. *arm of the settee.*) Simon, I had such a delicious idea—about our honeymoon. There is a place in Scotland—in the Hebrides—I should love to go there.

SIMON (*taken aback*). The Hebrides ? (*He takes a pace to her.*)

MARY ROSE. Yes ! We once went to it when I was little. Isn't it funny, I had almost forgotten about it and then suddenly I saw it quite clearly as I was sitting up there in the dark. (*A slight pause. Then, innocently.*) Of course, the little old woman came and pointed it out to me. *Isn't* she a queer one !

(*This is the sort of strange remark* MR. *and* MRS. MORLAND *have warned him about and* SIMON *is disturbed. She is almost in a trance.*)

SIMON (*after a pause*). Mary Rose. (*Another slight pause.*) Mary Rose !

(*She stands and moves to him.*)

There are only yourselves and the three maids in the house, aren't there ?

MARY ROSE (*surprised, for she has already forgotten what she said*). You know there are ! Whatever makes you ask ?

SIMON (*cautiously*). There isn't a little old woman in the house, is there ?

MARY ROSE. A little old woman ! (*Completely puzzled.*) Who on earth do you mean ?

SIMON. It doesn't matter. (*He is secretly troubled, but doesn't let on. He crosses down* L. *and turns.*) What was there particular about that place in the Hebrides ?

MARY ROSE (*standing below the* R. *end of the settee*). Oh, the fishing for Father, and there was an island where I often—my little island ! I wonder if it misses me !

SIMON (*moving in a little*). I don't think we'll go there.

MARY ROSE. Why not ?

SIMON. I'm not keen on fishing, you see—on my honeymoon.

MARY ROSE (*moving to him at* L.C.). Of course there's that. But I should love though to show you the tree trunk and the rowan tree where I used to sketch while Father was in the boat. I expect he used to land me on the island because it was such a safe place !

(SIMON *shivers a little and looks up at the ceiling.*)

SIMON. Yes ! (*He embraces her protectingly.*) And yet I should like to go there—some day—and see that island.

MARY ROSE. Yes—let's ! Now I'll put on that bothersome jacket . . . (*She turns and runs up to the door up* L.C., *and kisses her hand to him there.*) Tyrant !

She exits. SIMON, *somewhat perturbed, sits at the* R. *end of the settee, frowning to himself. The little figure on the clock is seen striking the hour on the anvil, during which—*

The CURTAIN *falls.*

ACT II

SCENE.—*The Island*, 1894.

The scene is laid on the island, with a suggestion of water at the back, on which a real small rowing-boat, or part of one, can appear when required. On the backcloth we see the mainland, which is two hundred yards away.

Details of the stage setting must come later. For the present it is sufficient to indicate as prominent one Scotch fir much beaten by the winds. This tree's effect is sombre, but a gay touch is given to the scene by a rowan tree gleaming with red berries. There is a mossy bank, which we shall discover later is an old tree-stump overgrown with moss. Moss, stones and long grass are everywhere, the moss of different colours, which has a pretty effect. It is to be a rather lovely scene, yet with a rather austere Corot effect. The wings are a mass of thick brushwood and tall grass or reeds and trees; you can't reach this spot by land except by squeezing through them. It is a sunny August day.

MARY ROSE *is heard laughing gaily, and presently she and* SIMON *force their way through the brushwood on* L. *He is no longer in uniform; he is in suitable tweeds, knickerbockers, etc. She is also wearing serviceable garments but not tweed, something soft, of pretty but subdued colour, probably mauve, which must also be very simple and emphasize her youthfulness. More than four years have elapsed since the last act, and they are an exuberantly happy married pair.* MARY ROSE *is more wildly impulsive than ever.* SIMON *is an adoring husband, who likes to pit his matter-of-factness against her enthusiasms.*

MARY ROSE (*to* R.C., *looking round thrilled, and flinging down her hat*). I think—I think! I don't think at all, I'm quite sure!—*this is the place.* (*Breathless.*) Simon, kiss me—kiss me, quick. You promised to kiss me quick when we came to the place.

SIMON (*in his bantering way*). I'm not the man to break my word. (*He kisses her.*) At the same time, Mary Rose, I would point out to you that this is the third spot you have picked out as being the "place" and three times have I kissed you quick on that understanding. We can't go on like this.

(MARY ROSE *looks around, her back to the audience.*)

MARY ROSE. It was here—here! I told you of the big fir and the rowan tree.

SIMON (*to* L.C.). There were a fir and a rowan tree at each of the other places.

MARY ROSE (*triumphantly*). Not this fir—not this rowan!

SIMON. You have me there. (*He sits on a boulder* L.C.)

MARY ROSE (C.). Simon, I know I'm not clever, but you must admit I'm always right. (*She addresses the tree* R.C.) Darling rowan, you don't look a bit older. How do you think *I* am wearing ? I'll tell you a secret. (*Moving to the rowan, pulling a branch towards her.*) I'm *married* !

(*The rowan branch springs back into its place.*)

It didn't like that, Simon. It's jealous. (*Cajoling the branch.*) But I have been married for nearly four years—this is him— Lieutenant Simon Sobersides. (*With a sudden new thought.*) Oh !

SIMON (*with a groan*). What is it now ? (*He is beginning to smoke his pipe.*)

(*She moves up* R.C.)

MARY ROSE. That moss ! I feel sure there is a tree-stump beneath it—the very root on which I used to sit and sketch.

SIMON (*moving a little* R. *of* C., *and clearing away some moss*). It's a tree-stump right enough.

MARY ROSE (*kneeling above the tree-stump, helping*). I think, I think I cut my name on it with a knife.

SIMON. Yes, here it is. M A R—there it stops. It's always at the third letter that the blade breaks.

MARY ROSE. Dear stump ! (*Still kneeling above it.*) How I have missed you !

SIMON (*moving back to* L.C.). Don't you believe it, old tree-stump. You just came vaguely back to her mind because we happened to be in these parts. And what a trumpery island you prove to be ! About a hundred yards across !

MARY ROSE. Even if it's true, you needn't say it before them all. (*She turns again to the stump and speaks to it.*) Here is one for each year I have been away. (*She kisses it a number of times.*)

SIMON (*counting them*). Eleven. Go on, give it all the news. Tell it we don't have a house of our own yet.

MARY ROSE (*to the tree stump*). You see, dear, we live with my daddy and mother, because Simon is so often away at sea. But I have a much more wonderful secret than that. This *will* startle you. I—have—got—a—baby ! A girl ? No, thank you ! He is two years and nine months, and he says such beautiful things to me about loving me—— (*Anxiously to the rowan tree.*) Oh, rowan, do you think he means them ?

SIMON (*sitting back*). I distinctly heard it say, yes.

MARY ROSE (*looking off up* R., *at the mainland and starting up*). Oh !

SIMON. You needn't pretend you can see him.

MARY ROSE (*moving up* R.C. *a little*). I do. Don't you ? Something white. He is waving his bib to us.

(SIMON *rises and goes up* L. *of* MARY ROSE.)

C

SIMON. That's Nurse's cap.

MARY ROSE. Then he's waving it. How clever of him. (*She waves her hand.*) Now they've gone. By-bye, I'll see you in an hour. (*Turning to* SIMON.) Isn't it funny to think that this is the place where I used to wave to Father. (*Moving down.*) We *were* happy here.

SIMON. I'd be happier here if I wasn't so hungry. I wonder where Cameron is ? I see he's laid a fire. I suppose I had better have a shot at lighting it myself. (*He crosses* R. *to pick up a few twigs.*)

MARY ROSE. How can you think of food at such a time——?

SIMON. All very well, but you will presently be eating more than your share.

(*He begins preparations for a fire. A pause while* MARY ROSE *sits on the stump.*)

MARY ROSE. Do you know, Simon, I don't think Daddy and Mum like this island.

SIMON (*guardedly, though he has long ceased to credit the queer story*). Oh ? Why not ? (*He sometimes watches her covertly.*)

MARY ROSE. I don't know, but they never seem to want to speak of it.

SIMON. That's nothing ; forgotten it, I suppose. (*He crosses* L. *with the twigs.*)

MARY ROSE. I'll write to them this evening. (*Gleefully.*) They will be surprised to know we are here.

SIMON (*knowing that it would alarm them*). I wouldn't write from here. Wait till we cross to the mainland. (*He sits on the boulder* L.C. *and adds the twigs to* CAMERON'S *fire.*)

MARY ROSE. Why not from here ?

SIMON. Oh—no reason. But if they have any reason for disliking the place, perhaps they wouldn't like our coming. (*He wants to change the subject.*)

MARY ROSE. What reason could they have ?

SIMON. I can think of none.

MARY ROSE. For a long time you didn't seem to want to come yourself.

SIMON (*casually, as he rises*). Only because it was so difficult to get at. (*Crossing up* R., *above* MARY ROSE, *looking off* R.) I have always had it in my mind though that I should like to come and see this island.

MARY ROSE. Because I had been so fond of it ?

SIMON (*though he is really thinking of the queer story*). Of course !

MARY ROSE. To-day you wanted to come across without me. (*Half turning to him.*) Why was that ?

(*He smiles down at her, then picks up a twig or two.*)

SIMON. Did I ? Oh, that was merely because you seemed tired. I thought I might pull across and have a prowl round your little island by myself.

MARY ROSE (*rising, to* L. *of* SIMON). Thinking of me as a child on it ?

SIMON. Exactly. (*Crossing down and back to the fire.*) And about a dream your father once told me he had about it.

MARY ROSE (*following him with her eyes*). A dream ?

SIMON (*kneeling by the fire, his back to her*). He didn't call it that, but I see clearly now it must have been a dream. (*He really does think so.*)

MARY ROSE. You must tell me about it.

SIMON. Some day. (*To change the subject.*) I wonder where Cameron is. Ah ! (*Rising.*) I hear him coming. He's an odd fish. You know, I expected him to speak broad Scotch.

MARY ROSE. Not a Highlander, Simon, not a soft-voiced Highlander. They are very different.

SIMON. Ah—here he is at last ! (*He settles down by the fire.*)

MARY ROSE. Do be polite to him, dear, you know how touchy they are.

(*For nearly all the rest of the Act,* SIMON *and* MARY ROSE *are sitting on the ground. The boat with* CAMERON *draws in from up* L. *He is a gawky youth of twenty, or more, dressed as the poorest sort of ghillie, but proud, and with accomplishments. He speaks in the soft voice of the Highlander, which has nothing in common with lowland Scotch. He has fine courteous manners.*)

CAMERON (*from the boat*). Iss it the wish of Mr. Blake that I tie up the boat here ?

SIMON (*striking a match*). That's the idea. (*He sets the match to the fire. Smoke rises.*)

CAMERON. I am now tying up the boat according to Mr. Blake's wish. Iss it the wish of Mr. Blake that I should land ?

SIMON. Yes, yes, Cameron, with the luncheon.

CAMERON. I can give Mr. Blake the basket without landing.

SIMON. No—no—we like you almost as much as the luncheon.

(MARY ROSE *leaves the stump and sits on the ground* R. *of it.*)

CAMERON (*landing, fearfully*). Iss it the wish of Mr. Blake that I unpack the basket ? (*He puts down the basket on the tree-stump.*)

SIMON. We'll look after that if you bring a trout or two. I want you to show my wife, Cameron, how you cook fish by the water's edge.

CAMERON (*moving back toward the boat*). I will do it with pleasure. (*Checking, at up* L.C.) There iss one little matter ; it iss of small importance. You may haf noticed that I always address you as Mr. Blake. I notice that you always address me as Cameron. I take no offence. (*He moves away up* L.C.)

MARY ROSE. Oh, dear! I am sure I always address you as Mr. Cameron. (*She takes the basket from the tree-stump.*)

CAMERON (*checking again*). That iss so, ma'am. You may have noticed that I always address you as "ma'am." It is my way of indicating that I consider you a very genteel young matron, and of all such I am the humble servant. (*He turns up, then back again.*) In saying I am your humble servant I do not imply that I am not as good as you are. With this brief explanation, ma'am, I will now fetch the trouts. (*He goes up to the water's edge.*)

(MARY ROSE *spreads the cloth* R.C.)

SIMON (*kneeling* C., *on her* L., *helping to unpack*). That's one in the eye for me, but I'm hanged if I "mister" him!

MARY ROSE. Simon, do be careful. If you want to say anything to me that's dangerous, say it in French. (*Laying sandwiches, pickles and marmalade, etc.*)

(CAMERON, *in the boat, is washing two trout. As he speaks, the others look up towards him.*)

CAMERON. The trouts, ma'am, having been cleaned in a thorough and yet easy manner by pulling them up and down in the water, the next procedure iss as follows. (*He wraps each trout in a piece of paper, varnished to represent dampness, and dips them over the boat edge.*)

MARY ROSE (*to* SIMON). It looks like a conjuring trick. What is he doing now?

SIMON. He is soaking the paper. You watch.

(CAMERON *leaves the boat, coming to above the fire* L.C.)

CAMERON. I now place the soaking little parcels on the fire—(*he does so*)—and when the paper begins to burn it will be a sure sign that the trouts iss now ready, like myself, (*going up* C.) ma'am, to be your humble servants. (*He turns to the boat.*)

MARY ROSE. Don't go. (*She rises, to* C.)

CAMERON. If it is agreeable to Mistress Blake I would wish to go back to the boat.

MARY ROSE. Why?

(*A pause.* CAMERON *looks around uncomfortably.*)

It would be more agreeable to me if you would stay.

CAMERON. Then . . . (*he looks round*) I will remain against my better judgment. (*He moves away to up* L.).

SIMON. Good man—and look after the trout. It's the most heavenly way of cooking fish, Mary Rose.

CAMERON· (*leaning on the fir tree* L.). It iss a tasty way, Mr. Blake—but I would not use the word heavenly in this connection.

SIMON. I stand corrected. (*Tartly, rising.*) I must say——

MARY ROSE. Prenez garde, mon brave !

SIMON (*crossing* R., *below* MARY ROSE). Mon Dieu ! Qu'il est un drole ! (*Turning up* R. *of the tree-stump.*)

MARY ROSE (*turning to face* SIMON). Mais moi je l'aime ; il est tellement—— (*In English.*) What is the French for an original ?

SIMON (*in English*). That stumps me.

CAMERON. Colloquially *coquin* might be used, though the classic writers would probably say simply *un original*.

SIMON (*this staggers them—with a groan*). I say, this is serious. (*Sitting on the stump* R.C.) What was that book you were reading, Cameron, while I was fishing ?

CAMERON. It is a small Euripides I carry in the pocket, Mr. Blake.

SIMON (*taking a sandwich*). Latin, Mary Rose !

(*They both eat.*)

CAMERON (*from the tree up* L.). It may be Latin, but in these parts we know no better than to call it Greek.

SIMON. Sold again ! Come on, Erasmus, sit down and have pot-luck with us.

CAMERON. I thank you, Mr. Blake, but it would not be good manners for a paid man to sit with his employers.

MARY ROSE. When I ask you, Mr. Cameron ?

CAMERON (*doggedly*). It iss kindly meant, ma'am, but I haf not been introduced to you.

(SIMON *rises.*)

MARY ROSE. Oh, but—do let me. My husband, Mr. Blake —Mr. Cameron.

(*The two men bow.*)

CAMERON. (*At* L.C.) I am glad to make Mr. Blake's acquaintance. I hope he is ferry well.

SIMON. The same to you, Mr. Cameron. How do you do ? Lovely day, isn't it ?

CAMERON. It iss a fairly fine day.

(SIMON *is about to sit.*)

MARY ROSE. Simon ! (*She rises.*)

SIMON. Oh ! Do you know my wife ? Allow me—Mr. Cameron—Mrs. Blake.

(MARY ROSE *curtsies.*)

CAMERON. I am ferry pleased to make Misstress Blake's acquaintance. Iss Mistress Blake making a long stay in these parts ?

MARY ROSE. No, alas ! We go across to-morrow.

CAMERON. I hope the weather will be favourable.

MARY ROSE. Thank you. And now you know you are our guest. . . . (*She gives him sandwiches in a paper parcel.*)

CAMERON. I am much obliged. (*He looks at the sandwiches.*) Butcher meat ! This is very excellent.

MARY ROSE (*sitting* R.C.). This Scotch air gives one such an appetite.

CAMERON. I thank you for that. (*He moves up to* C.)

(SIMON *sits on the stump down* R.C. *Suddenly,* CAMERON *bursts into a surprising fit of laughter, that makes him human and even attractive.*)

Please to excuse my behaviour. You haf been laughing at me all this time, but you did not know I haf been laughing at myself also, though keeping a remarkable control over my features. I will now haf my laugh out, and then I will explain. (*He has another roar of laughter, then controls himself.*) I will now explain. I am not the solemn prig I haf pretended to you to be, I am really a fairly attractive young man, but I am shy and I had been guarding against your taking liberties with your employee, not because of myself, who am nothing, but because of the noble profession it is my ambition to enter.

MARY ROSE. Do tell us what that is.

CAMERON. It iss the Ministry. I am a student of Aberdeen University, and in the vacation I am a boatman, or a ghillie or anything you please to help to pay my fees.

SIMON. I honour you for that.

CAMERON. I am obliged to Mr. Blake. (*Moving in a little to* L.C.) And I may say, now that we know one another socially, that there is much in Mr. Blake which I am trying to copy.

SIMON. Something in *me* worth copying ! Hurrah !

CAMERON. It is not Mr. Blake's learning—he has not much learning, but I haf always understood the English manage without it. What I admire in Mr. Blake iss his ferry nice manners and general deportment.

(SIMON *bows.*)

In all of which I haf a great deal to learn yet, and I watch these things in Mr. Blake and take memoranda of them in a little notebook.

MARY ROSE. Mr. Cameron, do tell me that I am in your little notebook ?

CAMERON. You are not, ma'am, it would not be seemly in me. But it iss written in my heart—and also I have said it to my father—that I will remain a bachelor unless I can marry some lady who is ferry like Mrs. Blake.

SIMON. Why did I never think of saying that——

MARY ROSE. Is your father a crofter in the village ?

CAMERON. He iss, ma'am, when he is not at the University of Aberdeen.

SIMON. My stars ! Does he go there, too ?

CAMERON. He does so. We share a very small room between us.

SIMON. Father and son ! Is he going into the Ministry, too ?

CAMERON. Such iss not his purpose. When he has taken his degree he will return and be a crofter again.

SIMON. In that case I don't see what he is getting out of it.

CAMERON (*with dignity*). He is getting the grandest thing in the world out of it. He iss getting education.

SIMON. You make me feel small. I——

MARY ROSE (*suddenly*). The trout !

(CAMERON *puts his sandwiches down near the stump. The paper has begun to burn.* CAMERON *crosses to the fire and rescues the trout.* MARY ROSE *gives some plates to* SIMON.)

MARY ROSE (*as* CAMERON *brings the trout—across to* SIMON). They do look good !

SIMON. Mr. Cameron ? (*Offering him some.*)

CAMERON (*at up* L.C.). No, I thank you. I have lived on trouts most of my life. The butcher meat is more of an excellent novelty to me. (*He crosses to* R.C., *and picks up his sandwich.*)

MARY ROSE (*to* CAMERON). Do sit down, Mr. Cameron (*She takes a plate of trout from* SIMON.)

CAMERON. I am doing ferry well here, I thank you.

MARY ROSE. But, please !

CAMERON (*doggedly*). I will not sit on this island.

SIMON (*taking some bread and butter from* MARY ROSE). Hullo ! (*Curiously.*) Come, come, are you superstitious, you, who are going into the Ministry !

CAMERON. This island has a bad name, I haf never landed on it before.

MARY ROSE. Why, Mr. Cameron ? How extraordinary ! I was once staying near here long ago, when I was small, and I often came to the island.

CAMERON (*surprised*). Iss that so ? It wass not a chancey thing to do.

MARY ROSE. Oh, but it's a darling island. (*She is eating the trout.*)

CAMERON. That iss the proper way to speak of it.

MARY ROSE. I am sure I never heard a word against it. Have you, Simon ?

SIMON (*guardedly*). Perhaps a little. They tell me in the village that its Gaelic name has an odd meaning—" The Island that Likes to be Visited "—but there's nothing terrifying in that.

MARY ROSE. The name is new to me, Mr. Cameron. I think it's sweet.

CAMERON. As to its being sweet, Mistress Blake, that iss as it may be.

SIMON. What is there against the island ?

CAMERON. For one thing they are saying it has no right to be here at all. It wass not always here, so they are saying. Then one day it wass here.

SIMON. That little incident happened before your time, I should say, Mr. Cameron.

CAMERON. It happened before the time of anyone now alive, Mr. Blake.

SIMON. I thought so. And does the island ever go away for a bit in the same way ?

CAMERON. There are some who are saying that it does.

SIMON. But you have not seen it on the move yourself ?

CAMERON (*with dignity*). I am not always watching it, Mr. Blake.

SIMON. Anything else against it ?

CAMERON. Then there iss the birds. These trees would be very nice for them—but no one has ever seen a bird on this island. (*Moving a little nearer.*) It's name iss against it for another thing, for, mark you, Mistress Blake, an island that had visitors would not need to want to be visited—and why has it not visitors ? Because they are afraid to visit it.

MARY ROSE. Whatever are they afraid of ?

CAMERON. That iss what I say to them. Whateffer are you afraid of, I say.

MARY ROSE. But what are *you* afraid of, Mr. Cameron ?

CAMERON (*standing up stage, a little L. of C.*). The same thing that they are afraid of. There are stories, ma'am.

MARY ROSE. Do tell us. (*She moves nearer SIMON, sitting below the tree stump*). Simon, wouldn't it be lovely if he would tell us some real eerie Highland stories !

SIMON (*rising*). Oh, I don't know. They mightn't be pretty. (*To CAMERON.*) I warn you, my friend, I'm not a sympathetic listener. You'll find me a bit of a cynic about your island.

MARY ROSE. Please, Mr. Cameron, I love to have my blood curdled.

CAMERON. There iss many stories. There is that one of the boy who was brought to this island—and they are saying that he was no older than your baby.

SIMON. What happened to him ?

CAMERON. No one knows, Mr. Blake. His people they were gathering rowans and when they looked round he was gone.

SIMON. Lost ?

CAMERON. He could not be found. He was never found.

MARY ROSE. Never ! How dreadful ! Had he fallen into the water ?

CAMERON. That iss a good thing to say, that he had fallen into the water. (*He moves up and looks off* L.) That iss what I say.

SIMON. But you don't believe it ?

CAMERON (*without turning*). I do not.

MARY ROSE. What do the people in the village say ?

CAMERON (*turning*). *Some* say he is on the island still.

SIMON. This hop, skip and a jump of an island ! What do the wise ones say ? What does your father say ?

CAMERON (*coming in a pace or two*). He thinks they are not always here but that they come and go.

SIMON. They ! Who are *they* ?

CAMERON (*looking away, uncomfortably*). I do not know. (*A little down* L.C.)

MARY ROSE. At any rate, the child must have wandered away. How could his people let him ?

CAMERON (*turning to* MARY ROSE). How could they prevent it, ma'am ? He had heard the call of the island.

SIMON (*putting down his plate*). I am curious. Let's get at the meaning of this if it has a meaning. How can the island " call " ?

CAMERON (*uncomfortably*). I do not know. (*He looks down, pressing out a smouldering twig with his foot.*)

SIMON. Do you know anyone who has heard the call ?

CAMERON. I do not. (*He looks across at* SIMON.) No one can hear it but those for whom it is meant.

MARY ROSE. But if that child heard it, the others must have heard it also—they were with him.

CAMERON. They heard nothing. (*He moves* C., *puts one foot up on a boulder, leaning on his knee.*) This is how it is. I might be standing close to you, Mrs. Blake, as it were here, and you there, and I might hear it, very loud, terrible or soft whispering —no one knows—but I would have to go, and you would not have heard a sound.

MARY ROSE (*rising, to* L. *of* SIMON). Dear, isn't it creepy ? (*She puts her arm across his shoulder.*)

SIMON. I expect we could soon pick holes in it. How long ago is this supposed to have happened, you credulous Highlander ?

CAMERON. It happened before I was born, Mr. Blake.

SIMON (*smiling*). I thought so !

MARY ROSE. Simon, don't make fun of my island. (*Turning*

to CAMERON.) Do you know any more stories about it, Mr. Cameron ?

CAMERON. It may be so that I do and it may be so that I do not—but I will not tell them if Mr. Blake says things the island might not like to hear.

SIMON. Not " chancey," I suppose ?

CAMERON. That iss so.

MARY ROSE (*turning to* SIMON). Simon ! Promise you will be careful.

SIMON. Well, go ahead, Cameron.

(MARY ROSE *sits below and* L. *of* SIMON, *facing* CAMERON.)

CAMERON. This story is of a young English miss, and they are saying she was about ten years of age.

MARY ROSE. Not so much younger than I was when I came here. How long ago was it ?

CAMERON. I think it is twelve years ago this summer.

MARY ROSE. Simon, it must have been just one year after I was here !

(SIMON *rises, having become uneasy because he realizes that it is her story that is coming.*)

SIMON (*getting on his knees, and preparing to pack the basket*). Very likely, but I say, we mustn't stay gossiping here. We must be getting back. Did you bail out the boat ?

CAMERON. I did not, but I will do it now, if such iss Mr. Blake's wish. (*He turns to move up* L.C.)

MARY ROSE (*rising*). The story first. I won't go without the story.

CAMERON (*turning back*). Well, then, the father of this miss he was fond of the fishing, and he sometimes landed the little maid on the island while he fished round it from the boat.

MARY ROSE (*to* SIMON). Listen to that ! Just as Father used to do with me ! (*She sits on the tree-stump.*)

SIMON. I daresay lots of bold tourists come over here—don't they ?

CAMERON. That iss so—if ignorance is boldness, and sometimes . . .

SIMON. Quite so, but I really think we must be starting. (*He is about to rise.*)

MARY ROSE. No, dear. (*To* CAMERON.) Please.

(SIMON *rises and moves up* R. *of* MARY ROSE. CAMERON *resumes his former attitude.*)

CAMERON. One day the father pulled over for his little one as usual. He saw her from the boat, she was sitting on the island, and it is said she kissed her hand to him. Then in a. moment more he reached the island, but she was gone.

MARY ROSE. Gone ?

CAMERON. She had heard the call of the island though no sound came to *him.*

MARY ROSE. Doesn't it make one shiver !

(SIMON *drops down a pace or two.*)

CAMERON. My father was one of the searchers. For many days they searched.

ᐧ MARY ROSE. But it would not take many minutes to search this little island.

CAMERON. They searched, ma'am, long after there was no sense in searching.

MARY ROSE. What a curdling story ! (*Rising, she moves down* L. *of* SIMON.) Darling, it might have been me. Is there any more ?

CAMERON. There iss more. It was about a month afterwards —her father was walking on the mainland, over there—and he saw something moving on the island. All in a tremble, ma'am, he came across in the boat, and it was his little miss.

MARY ROSE. Alive ?

CAMERON. Yes, ma'am.

MARY ROSE. He got her again. I am so glad, but it rather spoils the mystery.

SIMON (*curious to know how she feels about it*). How, Mary Rose ?

MARY ROSE. Because, of course, she could tell them what happened, stupid. Whatever had it been ?

CAMERON (*straightening up*). It iss not so easy as that, Mistress Blake. She did not know that anything had happened. She thought she had been parted from her father for but an hour.

MARY ROSE. Dear ! (*She takes* SIMON's *hand and he embraces her.*)

SIMON (*to* CAMERON). You and your bogies and kelpies and wraiths, you man of the mists !

MARY ROSE (*smiling to* SIMON). Don't be alarmed, Simon ; I was only pretending to believe.

CAMERON. That iss the wise thing to do when you are on the island. I believe it all when I am here, though I turn the cold light of remorseless reason on it when I am in Aberdeen.

SIMON (*chaffing as he crosses* L., *feeling in his pockets for his pipe*). Is that " chancey," my friend ? An island that has such extraordinary powers could surely send its call to Aberdeen or farther.

CAMERON (*troubled*). I had not thought of that. That may be ferry true. (*He turns up towards the boat.*)

SIMON (*down* L.). Beware, Mr. Cameron, lest some day when you are preaching far from here the call may pluck you out of the very pulpit and bring you back to the island in one jump.

CAMERON (*looking at* SIMON). I do not like Mr. Blake's talk. I will now go and bail the boat.

(*He goes and pushes the boat off, out of sight.*)

MARY ROSE (*sitting on the stump* R., *deliciously thrilled*). Suppose it were true, Simon ?

SIMON (*moving up* C.). But it isn't.

MARY ROSE. No, of course not, but if it had been, how awful for the girl when her father told her.

SIMON (*studying her cautiously as he fills his pipe*). Perhaps he never told her. He may have thought it wiser not to disturb her.

MARY ROSE. Poor girl ! Yes, I suppose that would have been best. And yet—it was taking a risk.

SIMON. How ?

MARY ROSE. Well, not knowing what had happened she might come back and—and be caught again ! (*She rises, to* C., *and looks around.*) Little island, I don't think I like you to-day.

SIMON. If she ever comes back, let's hope it is with an able-bodied husband to protect her.

MARY ROSE. Nice people, husbands. (*Luxuriating in pretended shudders.*). You won't let them catch *me*, will you, Simon ? (*Putting her hands on his shoulders.*)

SIMON. Let 'em try ! (*He puts his pipe away, not having lit it.*) And now to pack up the remnants, (*in burlesque, to make her bright*) and escape from the scene of the crime. (*He begins to do so.*) We'll never come back again, Mary Rose, I'm too frightened.

(*They kneel side by side and start to pack up the picnic things.*)

MARY ROSE. It's a shame to be funny about my island. (*To the island.*) You poor lonely island. (*She touches the tree-stump affectionately.*) I never knew about your liking to be visited—and I dare say this is my last visit. (*To* SIMON.) The last time of anything is always sad, don't you think ?

SIMON (*briskly, at his labours*). There must always be a last time, dearest dear.

MARY ROSE. Yes—I suppose—for everything. There must be a last time I shall see you, Simon. (*Half playfully, smoothing his hair.*) Some day I shall flatten this tuft for the thousandth time and then never do it again.

SIMON. Some day it won't be there, and I shall say " Good riddance."

(*She is whimsical rather than sad in what follows.*)

MARY ROSE. *I* shall cry.

SIMON. Goose ! (*He kisses her.*)

(*A slight pause.*)

MARY ROSE. Some day, Simon, you will kiss me for the last time.

SIMON. That wasn't the last time, at any rate! (*He kisses her again.*)

(*A strange trembling passes through* MARY ROSE'S *frame. She does not know what it means, but perhaps the audience feel that this is his last kiss.*)

(*Troubled.*) What is it ?

MARY ROSE. I don't know—something seemed to come over me.

SIMON (*brightly*). You and your last times! Let me tell you, madam, there will be a last time when you will see your baby.

MARY ROSE. Oh . . .!

SIMON (*hurriedly*). Well, he can't always be infantile, but the day after you have seen him for the last time as a baby you will see him for the first time as a young man. Think of that.

MARY ROSE. Often I think of that. The loveliest time of all will be when he is a man and takes *me* on his knee instead of my putting him on mine. Think of it ! How gorgeous ! (*With one of her sudden changes.*) Don't you think the saddest thing is that we seldom know when the last time *has* come ? We could make so much more of it.

SIMON. Oh, lor', no ! To know would spoil it all. I suppose I ought to stamp out the fire. (*He rises.*)

MARY ROSE (*rising*). Wait for Cameron. (*Quaintly.*) I want you to come and sit here on my tree-stump, Simon, and make love to me. (*She passes him across to her* R.)

(*He now sits on the tree-stump and she sits on the ground, nestling against him, on his* L.)

SIMON. What a life ! (*Teasingly.*) I believe I've forgotten the way.

MARY ROSE. Then I shall make love to you. (*She kneels up, quaintly, playing with his hair.*) Have I been a nice wife to you, Simon ? I don't mean always and always ; there was that awful day when I flung the butter-dish at you ! I *am* so sorry. But have I been a tolerably good wife on the whole—not a wonderful one, but a wife that would pass in a crowd ? (*She rams her head at him.*)

SIMON. Look here, if you are going to ram your head into me like that, you must take that pin out of your hair.

MARY ROSE. Have I been all right as a mother, Simon ? Have I been the sort of mother that Harry Morland Blake could both love and respect ?

SIMON (*judicially*). That's a very awkward question. You must ask Harry Morland Blake that.

MARY ROSE. Have I——?

SIMON. Shut up, Mary Rose! I know you, you'll be crying in a moment, and you don't have a handkerchief, for I wrapped it round the trout, whose head came off.

MARY ROSE. At any rate, Simon Blake, say you forgive me about the butter-dish.

SIMON. I am not so sure of that.

MARY ROSE (*sitting back on her heels*). And there were some other things—almost worse than the butter-dish.

SIMON. I should just say there were!

MARY ROSE (*kneeling erect*). Simon, how can you! There was nothing so bad as that.

SIMON (*with a groan*). I can smile at it now, but at the time I was a miserable man. I wonder I didn't take to drink.

MARY ROSE. Poor old Simon! (*Sitting back on her heels again.*) But how stupid you were, dear, not to understand.

SIMON. How could an ignorant young husband understand that it was a good sign when his wife flung the butter-dish at him?

MARY ROSE. You should have *guessed*.

SIMON. About Harry? How could I? I had always understood that when a young wife had a remarkably private statement to make to her husband, that she took him aside and went red—or white—and hid her head on his bosom—and whispered it. I admit I was hoping for that. (*He feels his head.*) But all I got was the butter-dish.

(*She butts him again with her head and then looks at him.*)

MARY ROSE. I suppose different women have different ways.

SIMON. I hope so. (*Severely.*) And that was a dastard trick you played me afterwards.

MARY ROSE. Which? Oh, that! Before *he* was born! (*Demurely.*) I just wanted you to be out of the way till he *was* born.

SIMON. I don't mean your getting me out of the house—sending me to Plymouth. The dastardliness was in not letting them tell me, when I got back, that—that he *was* born!

MARY ROSE (*gurgling*). It was very naughty of me. You remember, Simon, when you came in you tried to comfort me by saying it wouldn't be long now!—and I let you meander on, you darling.

SIMON. Gazing at me with solemn innocent eyes. You unutterable brat, Mary Rose!

MARY ROSE. You should have been able to read in my face how clever I had been. Oh, Simon, when I said at last: "Dearest, what *is* that funny thing in the basinette?" and you went and looked, *never* shall I forget your face!

SIMON. I thought at first, it was some baby you had borrowed.

MARY ROSE. I sometimes think so still. (*Childishly.*) I didn't, did I ?

SIMON. You are a droll one ! Always just when I think I know you at last I have to begin at the beginning again.

MARY ROSE (*suddenly*). Simon !

SIMON. Yes ?

(MARY ROSE *rises and moves* L.C., *and down a little.*)

MARY ROSE. If one of us had to—to go, and we could choose which one——

SIMON (*with a groan*). She's off again ! (*He rises and follows down to her.*)

MARY ROSE. No ! But *if*—I wonder which would be best. I mean for Harry, of course.

SIMON. Oh, I should have to hop it.

MARY ROSE (*clutching him*). Dear !

SIMON. Oh, I haven't popped off yet. (*He looks at her curiously.*) If I did go, I know your first thought would be : " The happiness of Harry mustn't be interfered with for a moment." You would blot me out for ever, Mary Rose, rather than he should lose one of his hundred laughs a day.

MARY ROSE (*guiltily*). Oh !

SIMON. It's true, isn't it ?

MARY ROSE. It's true at any rate that if I was the one to go, that's what I should like *you* to do. (*With a new thought.*) Oo ! (*She crosses* R., *below* SIMON.)

SIMON. What is it now ? Don't step on the marmalade.

MARY ROSE (*turning at down* R.). Simon, isn't life lovely ! I'm so happy, happy, happy ! Aren't you ? (*She moves up* R.C.)

SIMON. Rather ! (*He is tying up the marmalade jar.*)

MARY ROSE. But you can tie up marmalade ! (*Moving to him* L.C.) Why don't you scream with happiness ? One of us has got to scream.

SIMON (*putting the rest of the things in the basket*). Then I know which one it will be. Scream away, it will give Cameron the jumps.

(*The boat, with* CAMERON, *draws in up* L.C.)

(*Rising.*) There you are, Cameron. We are still safe, you see. You can count us—two. (*He folds the tablecloth.*)

CAMERON (*in the boat*). I am ferry glad.

(MARY ROSE *wanders up* R.C.)

SIMON (*moving up* L.C., *and handing* CAMERON *the luncheon basket*). Stay there and I'll stamp out the fire myself.

CAMERON. As Mr. Blake pleases.

SIMON (*turning at up* L.C.). Ready, Mary Rose ?

MARY ROSE. Yes.

(*While* SIMON *moves down stage, trying to kill the fire,* CAMERON *is reclining in the boat, reading his Euripides, and* MARY ROSE *has her farewell to the island.*)

(*Moving about.*)   Good-bye, old mossy seat ; good-bye, M A R —nice rowan.   Good-bye, little island, that likes too much to be visited.   (*She puts her arms round the tree up* R.)   Perhaps I'll come back when I am an old lady with wrinkles, and you won't know your Mary Rose.

SIMON (*looking about for smouldering twigs, stamping them out*). I say, dear, do dry up.   I can't help listening to you when I ought to be getting this fire out.

MARY ROSE. I won't say another word ! (*She holds her tongue—sitting on the stump.*)

SIMON.   Just as it seems to be out, sparks come again.   Do you think if I were to get some wet stones——?

(*He looks up and sees that she is whimsically holding her tongue with her hand.   They laugh at each other.*)

You child !

(*The organ-pipe begins.* SIMON *is then occupied for a little time in bringing wet stones from the loch and dumping them on the fire and watching the result.* CAMERON *is still in the boat reading.* MARY ROSE *is sitting demurely but gaily, holding her tongue, like a child.   But something else is happening.   The island has begun to " call " to* MARY ROSE. *The sound is like the wash of waves on some untrodden shore, with wind whistling through it and a strange moaning, got best, perhaps, from a great cry on a pipe. The organ pipe is accompanied after two or three seconds by wind and rain, and then the music is heard.   All effects increase in volume, with crescendo in the music, and cease suddenly when it reaches its climax.   As the music swells, the wind stops.*

It is mysterious and threatening and is at first as soft as a whisper, but it rapidly increases in volume till it is horribly loud. It is furtive, fearsome, seductive, but beneath it there is lovely music and calls to MARY ROSE *as if there were something very beautiful about the " call " which is trying to assert itself, but is largely drowned in the other more eerie sounds.   To the eye all is as placid and sunny as before.   We hear the call and* MARY ROSE *hears it, but* SIMON *and* CAMERON *continue as above, hearing nothing.   At first* MARY ROSE *continues sitting, only conscious of a sound, but soon she is like one mesmerized.   She has risen now.   Once one arm goes out to* SIMON *for help, but thereafter she is oblivious of his existence.   She is not frightened, but neither is there joy in her face.   She has a wrapt face.   When the storm is at its loudest, she passes* R. *through the brushwood out of sight,* R., *her arms outstretched.   Then the " call " dies away and there is silence—the island has got her.*)

SIMON (*kneeling on the ground by the fire, and addressing* MARY ROSE *as he thinks, but without looking at where he imagines her to be*). I think that makes it all right, and that we can leave it now. I don't see any sparks. (*Without looking up.*) You needn't be so silent as all that. (*He rises and looks round where she should be. Her absence merely makes him smile.*) Where have you got to ? (*He rises.*) I say, no hiding. We must really be going. Mary Rose ! (*A little disturbed.*) Dearest, don't ! (*Anxiously, moving* R.) Mary Rose !

(*He disappears* R. *in search of her.* CAMERON *realizes there is trouble, but is reluctant to come ashore.* SIMON'S *voice is heard calling :*)

Mary Rose ! Mary Rose ! (*A slight pause, then in a panic-stricken tone.*) Mary Rose !

(CAMERON *has the courage to land.* SIMON *reappears and comes down* R.)

Cameron ! (*He moves up* O., *facing* CAMERON.) I can't find her !

CAMERON. Oh ! Mr. Blake——

(CAMERON'S *face shows what is in his mind and fills* SIMON *with dread.* SIMON, *beside himself, rushes off* R. *again, leaving* CAMERON *standing near the boat appalled. In silence the scene changes to moonlight to suggest the passing of time. We still see* CAMERON *standing affrighted. We do not see* SIMON *but from a distance we hear his cry, with increasing anguish :* " Mary Rose ! Mary Rose ! Mary Rose ! " *There is no music or any other sound from the time* MARY ROSE *goes off to the end of the act.*)

CURTAIN.

ACT III

Scene 1

Scene.—*The scene is the home of the Morlands again—the cosy room of Act I, Scene 2, but in* 1917.

In essentials it is as we saw it last, but there should be some minor changes, for twenty-eight years have passed since we saw it last. Thus the chintzes are more worn or have been replaced by others of a different pattern, and the curtains are faded. It is, however, still a bright and happy room, warm with geniality and homeliness. The time is a pleasant autumn afternoon just before twilight comes. Through the closed windows we see the apple tree, in its autumn fruit and foliage, but a pleasant sight still.

There is a bright fire burning, and round it sit MR. *and* MRS. MORLAND, *and* MR. AMY. *They are all over seventy now, but on the whole are well-preserved and full of vigour.* MRS. MORLAND, *who looks a greater dear than ever, is sitting at the* R. *end of the settee, so that her face is well seen by us. She is reading a copy of " Punch " with the help of a magnifying glass and is evidently finding it very funny as her face shows.* MR. AMY *is on her* L. *and* MR. MORLAND *is poking the fire.* MR. AMY, *who has been half asleep, wakes up and sees the silent laughter on* MRS. MORLAND'S *face, and nudges* MR. MORLAND *to draw his attention to it. She is unconscious that they are watching her. She looks up and catches them at it.*

MRS. MORLAND. Oh, you bad men!

MORLAND. What is it, Fanny?

MRS. MORLAND. It's this week's " Punch "—so very amusing!

AMY. Ah, " Punch "—it isn't what it used to be.

MORLAND. Nothing like.

MRS. MORLAND. I don't agree. You see if you can look at that without laughing.

(She gives " Punch " to AMY, *who tries to read, holding it at arm's length. A pause.)*

You're trying not to laugh.

*(*AMY *smiles.* MORLAND *takes the " Punch," reads, and is highly amused. All three guffaw.)*

MORLAND. I think I can say that I enjoy a joke as much as ever. *(He sits in the armchair below the fire, facing* R.*)*

MRS. MORLAND. You light-hearted old man!

MORLAND. Not so old, Fanny, my dear. Will you please to remember that I am two months younger than you.

MRS. MORLAND. How can I forget it when you have been casting it up against me all our married life.

MORLAND. Only occasionally, my dear, when you needed to be kept in order. (*To* AMY.) Fanny and I are seventy-one. You are a bit younger, George.

AMY. Oh, yes. Oh, dear yes!

MORLAND (*a little annoyed*). You never say *exactly* what your age *is*.

AMY. I'm in the sixties. I'm sure I have told you that before.

MORLAND. It seems to me you have been in the sixties longer than it is usual to be in them.

MRS. MORLAND (*warningly*). James!

MORLAND. No offence, George, I was only going to say that at seventy-one I certainly don't feel my age. How do you feel, George, at—at sixty-two? Do you feel your sixty-two years?

(*Louder, and leaning forward, as if* AMY *were a little deaf.*)

AMY (*testily*). I am more than sixty-two.

MORLAND (*with a shade of sarcasm*). Who would have thought it!

MRS. MORLAND (*as before*). James!

AMY. I certainly don't feel more than sixty-two. It was only last winter that I learned to skate!

MORLAND. I still go out with the hounds. You forgot to come last time, George.

AMY. If you are implying anything against my memory, James——

MORLAND. What do you say?

AMY. I was saying that I have never used glasses in my life.

MORLAND (*sharply, taking off his glasses*). If I wear glasses occasionally it certainly isn't because there is anything defective with my eyesight. But the type used by newspapers nowadays is so vile——

AMY. There I agree with you. Especially Bradshaw.

MORLAND (*not hearing him*). I say the type used by newspapers nowadays is vile. Don't you think so?

AMY. I have just said so. (*Pleasantly.*) You are getting very dull of hearing, James.

MORLAND. Me? I like that, George! Why I have constantly to shout to you nowadays.

AMY. What annoys me is not that you are a little deaf—you can't help that. But from the nature of your replies I often see that you are pretending to have heard what I said when you didn't. That's rather vain, James.

(MRS. MORLAND'S *attitude throughout the scene is that of a mother amused by two children and smiling to herself.*)

MORLAND (*rising in dudgeon and crossing* R. *to the bureau*). Vain ! Now you have brought this on yourself, George. I have got something here I might well be vain of. And I meant not to show it to you because it will make you squirm.

(AMY *rises and crosses to* L. *of the table.*)

It'll make you squirm.

(MRS. MORLAND " Ah'ems " *warningly.* MORLAND *produces a water-colour, unframed, from a drawer in the bureau, and moves up* R. *to above the table.*)

(*In answer to* MRS. MORLAND'S *signal.*) I didn't mean that, George. I'm sure you'll be delighted. What do you think of that ?

(*He displays the picture, and* AMY *examines it at arm's length.* MORLAND *attempts to take it.*)

I'll hold it out to you, as your arms are so short.

(AMY *is very annoyed. He indignantly refuses.*)

AMY. Very nice. What do you call it ? (*He hands the picture back.*)
MORLAND. Have you any doubts ? I haven't the slightest. I am as sure as that I am standing here that it's an early Turner.
AMY. Turner ! (*He sits* L. *of the table.*)
MORLAND (*giving the picture to* AMY, *who examines it with a glass*). What else, than a Turner, can it be ? Holman suggested a Girton or even a Dayes. Absurd ! Why Dayes was only a glorified drawing-master. (*Sitting.*) I flatter myself I can't make a mistake about a Turner. There's something about a Turner difficult to define, but unmistakable—an absolute something. It's a charming view, too—Kirkstall Abbey obviously.
AMY. Rivaulx, I'm sure.
MORLAND. I say Kirkstall.

(MRS. MORLAND *gives a gentle* " Ah'em.")

(*Taking up the illustrated paper.*) You may be right—the place doesn't matter.
AMY. Now, there's an engraving of Rivaulx in this copperplate book we were looking at. Where is it ? Wait a minute. (*He turns up the magazine.*) I've got it—Rivaulx. Why, this is very funny. It's an engraving of this very picture and—— (*He takes a magnifying glass from his pocket.*) Hello, hello, hello ! It's signed E. Dayes.

(MORLAND, *in a tremble, examines the picture close to his eyes and gets a shock.*)

I wouldn't eat it, James. So it's the drawing-master after all!
I'm sorry you have had this disappointment, James.

MORLAND (*rising*). I—I—I—— (*He meets* MRS. MORLAND'S
warning glance.) Fanny, I won't——sixty-two! You sixty-
two! (*He goes up* R.)

(AMY, *affronted, rises, and turns away, then up* O., *facing*
MORLAND.)

AMY. This is very painful. Your chagrin I can well understand, but surely your sense of manhood—I am sorry that I
have overstayed my welcome. I bid you good afternoon. I
thank you, Mrs. Morland, for your unvarying hospitality.

(MORLAND *has turned up to the windows, staring out.*)

MRS. MORLAND (*as in Act I—rises*). I shall see you into your
coat, George.

AMY. I thank you, Mrs. Morland, I require no one to see
me into my coat.

(AMY *struts off, and* MRS. MORLAND *blandly follows.* MORLAND
*throws the picture down on the table ; then, on second thoughts,
picks it up, goes down and puts it away in the bureau drawer.*
AMY *returns, wearing his coat.* MRS. MORLAND *leading him.*
She moves to L.O., *curtsies to* MORLAND, *then to* AMY, *who yields.*)

(*Above the table, with his hand out.*) I can't leave this friendly
house in wrath, James.

(MRS. MORLAND *moves to up* L.O.)

MORLAND (R. *of the table*). I'm an irascible old beggar, George.
What I should do without you——

(*As they shake hands :*)

AMY. Or I without you. Or either of us without that little
old dear (*looking at* MRS. MORLAND), to whom we are a never-
failing source of mirth.

(*She curtsies.*)

Good day again. Tell Simon when he comes that I shall be in
to see him to-morrow. Good-bye, Fanny. I suppose you think
of the pair of us as in our second childhood ?

MRS. MORLAND (*muffler bus.*). Not your second, George. I
have never known any men who have quite passed their first——

(AMY *shakes his fingers at her jocularly and goes, followed up to the*
door by MORLAND.)

MORLAND (*filling his pipe and moving to* R. *of the table*). He's
a good fellow, but funny how touchy he is about his age. And
he has a way of falling to sleep while one is talking to him.

Mrs. Morland. He's not the only one of you who does that.

(*She stands by the window. Dusk is beginning to come now. He moves up beside her, on her* R.)

Morland. Eh ? What are you thinking about, Fanny ?

Mrs. Morland. I was thinking about the apple tree, and that you've given the order for its destruction.

Morland. It must come down. It is becoming a danger—might fall on someone down there any day.

Mrs. Morland. I quite see it has to go. (*Reminiscent, but not emotional.*) But, her tree ! How often she made it a sort of ladder from this room to the ground.

Morland. Who ? Oh, yes, of course. Did she used to climb the apple tree ? Yes, I think she did. (*He moves away from the window, to above the table.*)

Mrs. Morland (*kindly*). Had you forgotten that also, James ?

Morland (*doleful*). I'm afraid I forget a lot of things.

Mrs. Morland (*softly*). Just as well.

Morland (*turning towards her*). It's so long since she—how long is it, Fanny ?

Mrs. Morland (*staring out through the windows*). Twenty-five years—quarter of a century. It will soon be dark. I can see the twilight running across the fields ; (*moving down towards the settee*) draw the curtains, dear.

(Morland *does so, and turns on the light by the switch at the door. The clock strikes the half-hour.*)

(*Sitting on the* L. *end of the settee.*) Simon's train must be nearly due, isn't it ?

Morland (*moving to* R. *of the settee*). In ten minutes or so. Did you forward his telegram ?

Mrs. Morland. No. I thought he would probably get it sooner if I kept it here. (*She takes up her knitting and sits facing* R.)

Morland. I dare say. (*He moves behind the settee, troubled, takes the knitting out of her hand and drops it on the settee beside her.*)

Mrs. Morland (*turning a little, on the settee*). What is it, dear ?

Morland (*contrite, bending towards her*). I am afraid I was rather thoughtless about the apple tree, Fan.

Mrs. Morland (*smiling*). Oh, no.

Morland. Yes, I hurt you.

Mrs. Morland (*brightly*). Such nonsense ! Have another smoke, James. (*She picks up her knitting.*)

Morland (*doggedly, moving round* R. *of the settee*). I will not have another smoke. I'm to give up smoking for a month as a punishment to myself. (*He crosses below the settee, to the fire.*)

MRS. MORLAND (*watching him fondly*). Foolish man !

MORLAND (*turning at the fireplace*). Why is it my heart is not broken ? If I had been a man of real feeling, my heart would have broken twenty-five years ago—just as yours did. ✓

MRS. MORLAND. Mine didn't, dear.

MORLAND. In a way it did. At the time I thought I could never raise my head again, but there's a deal of the old Adam in me still.

MRS. MORLAND. Well, as for the old Adam in you—dear Adam, there is still something of the old Eve in me. Our trip to Switzerland two years ago with Simon, I enjoyed every hour of it.

MORLAND (*crossing to* L.C., *and sitting* R. *of* MRS. MORLAND). Your brightness hasn't been all pretence ?

MRS. MORLAND. No, indeed. I have passed through the valley of the shadow, dear, but I can say thankfully that I have come out again into the sunlight. (*A little tremulously.*) I suppose it is all to the good that as the years go by, the dead should recede farther from us.

MORLAND. Some say they don't.

MRS. MORLAND. You and I know better, James.

MORLAND. Up there in the misty Hebrides, I dare say they think of her as on the island still. (*A slight pause.*) Fan, how long is it since—since you half thought *that* yourself ?

MRS. MORLAND (*putting down her work*). So many years ago. (*Gazing out front.*) Perhaps not the first year—I did cling for a time——

(*She pauses. He pats her hand kindly. She sighs and takes up her work again.*)

It's all unfathomable. It's as if Mary Rose was just something beautiful that you and I and Simon had dreamt together. You have forgotten much, but so have I. Even that room— (*looking towards the door up* L.C.) that was hers so long—even during all her short married life—I often go into it now without remembering that it was hers.

MORLAND (*rising*). It's strange ! (*Moving to above the table.*) It's rather terrible. (*A little bitterly.*) You're pretty nigh forgotten, Mary Rose !

MRS. MORLAND. You know that isn't true, dear. But Mary Rose belongs to the past, and we have to live in the present—for a very little longer. Even if we could drag her back to tell us what these things mean, I think it would be a shame.

MORLAND. Yes, I suppose so. (*Moving to* R. *of the settee.*) Do you think Simon is a philosopher about it also ?

MRS. MORLAND. Don't be bitter, James, to your old wife. Simon was very fond of her. He was a true lover.

MORLAND (*turning away to* L. *of the table, the bitterness creeping back*). Was ! Was ! Is it all " was " about Mary Rose ?

MRS. MORLAND. It just had to be. He had all the clever ones of the day advising, suggesting, probing. He went back to the island every year for a long time.

MORLAND (*sitting* L. *of the table*). Yes, and then he missed a year, and that somehow ended it.

MRS. MORLAND. He never married again. Most men would. (*She puts down her work and rises, smoothing her dress.*)

MORLAND. He's mightily keen on his work. What a jolly hearty fellow he is.

MRS. MORLAND (*crossing* R. *to above the table*). If you mean he isn't heart-broken, he isn't. Mercifully the wound has healed.

MORLAND. I'm not criticizing, Fan. I suppose anyone who came back after twenty-five years—however much they had been loved—it might—we—would we know what to say to them, Fanny ?

MRS. MORLAND (*laying her hand on his* R. *shoulder*). Don't, James ! (*Looking at the clock.*) Simon is late, isn't he ? (*She rises.*)

MORLAND. Very little. (*He rises, looks at his watch, and crosses* L.) I heard the train a short time ago—and he might be here—just—if he had the luck to find a cab—but if he is walking across the fields. . . .

MRS. MORLAND. Listen !

MORLAND (*checking, and turning at* L.C.). Yes, wheels ! That's probably Simon. He had got a cab.

(MRS. MORLAND *goes up to the window and peeps out.*)

MRS. MORLAND. I do hope he won't laugh at me for having lit a fire in his room !

MORLAND (*with pretended gravity, at the fireplace with his back to her*). I hope you put him out some bed socks.

MRS. MORLAND (*deceived*). Do you think he would let me ? (*She turns and sees he is laughing at her.*) You wretch !

(*She opens the door* R., *and exits.*)

(*Off.*) Is that you, Simon ? Yes, it is.

SIMON (*unseen*). Ahoy there !

(*Enter* SIMON, *carrying* MRS. MORLAND. *He is in a great-coat and mufti. He looks his fifty-three years or so, grizzled, grey hair and not very much of it—the tuft gone—heavier, more commanding, full of vigour, a manly fellow—could be stern, but is at present frank and expansive.*)

MRS. MORLAND (*at* C.). Let me down, you great bear.

SIMON. Come aboard, sir. (*He puts her down and salutes.*)

MRS. MORLAND. You know how I hate to be rumpled. (*She is in high delight.*)

MORLAND. Not she—loves it ! Always did !

SIMON. Bless you, they're all alike in that way.

(*He takes off his great-coat,* MRS. MORLAND *takes it, settles* SIMON *on the settee, then carries the coat to the chair above the table.* SIMON *rubs his hands together.*)

MRS. MORLAND (*fussing about him*). How cold your hands are. Come nearer to the fire. (*She urges him to the* L. *end of the settee, and sits on his* R.)

MORLAND. He's looking fit, though! (*He sits in the chair below the fire.*)

SIMON (*warming his hands*). I am fit.

MRS. MORLAND. So nice to have you again. You do like roast duck, don't you ? Your train was late, wasn't it ?

SIMON. Only a few minutes. I made a selfish bolt for the only cab, and got it.

MORLAND. We thought you might be walking across the fields.

SIMON. No, but two people who got out of the train did. One of them a lady. I thought something about her walk was familiar to me, but it was darkish, and I didn't make her out.

MRS. MORLAND (*rising*). Bertha Colinton, I expect. (*Moving to the table* R.C.) She *was* in London. (*She tidies the table.*)

SIMON. I dare say. If I had thought it was Mrs. Colinton I would have offered her a lift. (*More important.*) Mother, I have news ; I have got the " Bellerophon."

MRS. MORLAND (*turning to him, ecstatically*). The very ship you wanted !

SIMON. Rather !

(MRS. MORLAND *goes on tidying.*)

MORLAND. Bravo, Simon.

SIMON. It's like realizing the ambition of one's life. I'm one of the lucky ones, I admit.

MORLAND (*mocking*). Beastly life, a sailor's.

SIMON. Beastly ! I've loathed it ever since I slept in the old " Britannia," with my feet out at the port-hole to give them air. We all slept that way. Must have been a pretty sight from the water ! Oh, a beast of a life, but I wouldn't exchange it for any other life in the world.

MRS. MORLAND. Simon, I had forgotten. There's a telegram for you.

SIMON. Avaunt !

MRS. MORLAND. I put it in your room.

(*She exits up* L.C.)

SIMON. I do hope it's not recalling me. I had hoped for at least five clear days.

(MRS. MORLAND *returns and gives him the telegram.*)

Mrs. Morland. We didn't open it.

Simon (*to* Morland, *as he rises*). Two to one it's recalling me.

Mrs. Morland. It came two days ago.

Simon (*turning to her, surprised*). Two days ago! I wonder now——

Mrs. Morland. I don't like them, Simon, never did; they've broken so many hearts.

Simon. They've made many a heart glad, too. It may be from my Harry at last. Mother, do you think I was a bit harsh to him?

Mrs. Morland. I sometimes think you were, my son. Open it, Simon.

(Simon *opens the telegram, reads it, and receives a dreadful shock.* Mrs. Morland *is frightened by the expression on his face.* Morland *rises, and moves up a pace, before the fire, takes the telegram, and reads.* Mrs. Morland *breaks the pause.*)

Mrs. Morland. It can't be as bad as that! We are all here, Simon. (*Appealing.*) James!

Morland. Can't be! Can't be!

(Simon's *first thought when he comes to, is for* Mrs. Morland. *He puts her very lovingly into the settee.*)

Simon (*sitting beside her, he smoothes her cheeks and is everything that is kind and manly*). It's all right, Mother. Don't you be afraid. It's good news, you're a brave one, you've come through a lot, you'll be brave for another minute, won't you?

(*She nods.*)

Mother dear, it's Mary Rose!

Morland (*dazed*). It can't be true! It's too good to be true!

Mrs. Morland (*softly*). Is my Mary Rose alive?

Simon (*still solicitous for her*). It's all right—all right. I wouldn't say it, would I, if it wasn't true. Mary Rose has come back. (*He takes the telegram from* Morland.) It's from Cameron. You remember who he was. He's minister there now. Hold my hand, and I'll read it. (*He reads.*) " Your wife has come back. She was found to-day on the island. I am bringing her to you. She is quite well, but you will all have to be very careful."

Mrs. Morland. Simon, can it be?

Simon. I believe it absolutely. Cameron wouldn't deceive me.

Morland. He might be deceived himself. He was a mere acquaintance.

Simon. I'm sure it's true. He knew her to look at as well as any of us.

Morland. But after twenty-five years!

SIMON.   Do you think *I* wouldn't know her after twenty-five years ?

MRS. MORLAND.   My—my—she will be—very changed.

SIMON.   However changed, Mother, wouldn't I know my Mary Rose at once ? Her hair may be as grey as mine—her face—her little figure—her pretty ways—though they were all gone, don't you think I would know Mary Rose at once ! (*He is suddenly stricken with a painful thought—and rises slowly.*) Oh, my God, I saw her, and I didn't know her.

MRS. MORLAND.   Simon !

SIMON (*crossing slowly to* C.).   It had been Cameron with her. (*He turns to them.*) They must have come in my train, Mother. It was she I saw going across the fields—her little walk when she was excited, half a run, I recognized it, but I didn't remember it was hers.

MORLAND (*comforting*).   It was getting dark.

SIMON (*almost in a whisper*).   Mary Rose is coming across the fields !

(*He goes out* R. *A pause. The old man and woman are feeling their age. MORLAND goes slowly to the window, and peers out through the curtains. MRS. MORLAND stares into the fire, her hands on her lap.*)

MORLAND.   It's rather dark.   I—I shouldn't wonder though there was a touch of frost to-night. (*After a little pause.*) I wish I was more use.

(*This is all he can say. He comes down again below the settee, lays his hand on her shoulder a moment, and then passes her, to the fire, standing on her* L. *as* CAMERON *enters* R. CAMERON *is already quite elderly in appearance. He is grave, and troubled— a good man. He wears a heavy overcoat and muffler, which prevents our seeing that he is in Scotch clerical dress.* MRS. MORLAND *rises.*)

Mr. Cameron ?

CAMERON.   Yes.

MRS. MORLAND.   Tell us quickly, Mr. Cameron, is it true ?

CAMERON (*standing* C.).   It iss true, ma'am. Mr. Blake met us and he iss with her now. I hurried on to tell you the things which were necessary. It iss good for her you should know them at once.

MRS. MORLAND (*quickly*).   Please.

(*She holds* MORLAND'S *arm. He pats her hand.*)

CAMERON.   You must be prepared to find her—different.

MRS. MORLAND (*sitting again on the settee*).   We are all different. Her age——

CAMERON (*sitting in the chair* L. *of the table*).   I mean, Mrs.

Morland, different from what you expect. She is not different as we are different. She is just as she was the day she went away.

(MRS. MORLAND *shrinks back a little*.)

These five-and-twenty years, she thinks they were just an hour in which Mr. Blake had left her in some incomprehensible jest.

MRS. MORLAND (*turning to* MORLAND). James! Just as it was before!

MORLAND (*to* CAMERON). But when you told her?

CAMERON. She will not have it.

MRS. MORLAND. She must have seen how much older you are.

CAMERON. She does not know me, ma'am, as the boy who was with her that day. When she did not recognize me I thought it best—she was so troubled already—not to tell her.

MORLAND. But now that she has seen Simon. His appearance—his grey hair—when she saw him she would know.

CAMERON. I am not sure. (*Glancing* R. *to the door*.) It is dark out there.

MORLAND. She must know that he would never have left her and come home.

CAMERON. That secretly troubles her, but she will not speak of it. There is some terrible dread lying on her heart.

MRS. MORLAND (*stricken*). I know! Harry! (*She rises*.) James, if she should think that Harry is still a child.

CAMERON. I never heard what became of the boy.

MRS. MORLAND. Poor Harry! (*Indicating the door up* L.C.) That room was his nursery. He was very high-spirited! He ran away to sea when he was twelve years old. We have had a few letters from Australia—very few—we don't know where he is now.

MORLAND (*moving to* R. *of the settee*). How was she found, Mr. Cameron?

CAMERON. Two men fishing from a boat saw her. She was asleep on the shore at the very spot where Mr. Blake made a fire so long ago. There was a rowan tree beside it. At first they were afraid to land, but they did. They said there was such joy on her face as she slept that it was a shame to waken her.

MORLAND. Joy? But when they *did* waken her?

CAMERON. She knew nothing.

MRS. MORLAND. Nothing——!

(*She puts her hands over her face.* CAMERON *rises and moves down* R.)

MORLAND. I have sometimes thought——

(*He stops speaking, for he has heard a door below.* MRS. MORLAND *crosses* MORLAND, *to* C. *Then we hear* MARY ROSE *clattering up*

*the stairs just as before. If this is properly done in Act I, it
should have a strange effect now. MORLAND moves down below
the settee. The door opens and MARY ROSE runs in. She is just
as we saw her last—the same age and in the same clothes, much
faded. SIMON enters after her.)*

MARY ROSE. Mother !

*(She runs to her mother in the old impetuous way. MRS. MOR-
LAND'S arms are stretched out to her. But before they meet, the
change in her mother's appearance startles MARY ROSE, and she
stops short. All this scene is very still and quiet.)*

MARY ROSE. What is it ?
MRS. MORLAND. My love.

(But MARY ROSE shrinks back.)

MORLAND *(taking a pace towards her).* Mary Rose !
MARY ROSE *(running down L. to him).* Dad !

*(SIMON moves past MRS. MORLAND to below the R. end of the settee,
then stops. He sees that MORLAND has the same effect on MARY
ROSE. She shrinks back, and then turns timidly to SIMON, her
R. hand stretched out, more wondering than afraid.)*

What is it, Simon ? *(Until this moment she has not seen the
change in him. Now she sees the grey hair and shrinks back again.)*
SIMON *(taking her in his arms).* My beloved wife.

*(MARY ROSE rests, contented in his arms for a moment, but soon
softly disengages herself, for there is something on her mind.
She moves up to MRS. MORLAND.)*

MRS. MORLAND *(petting her).* Mary Rose—Mary Rose.
MORLAND *(feebly, unable to cope with the situation).* We are
so glad you—had you a comfortable journey, Mary Rose ?

(MARY ROSE turns to look at him.)

You would like a cup of tea, wouldn't you ?

(There is no response.)

Is there anything I can do ?

*(MARY ROSE'S eyes go from him to the door up L.C. She wants to
rush into that room, but dare not. She runs back to MORLAND
down L.)*

MARY ROSE *(coaxingly).* Tell me !
MORLAND. Tell you what, dear ?

*(MARY ROSE turns her face up to the door L.C. MRS. MORLAND
and SIMON involuntarily look in the same direction. MARY
ROSE leaves MORLAND and moves swiftly across to CAMERON.)*

MARY ROSE (*appealingly to him*). You . . . ?

(CAMERON *touches her hand, and turns away.* MARY ROSE *retreats a step, turns, and goes up to* R. *of* SIMON *and strokes his arm, cajolingly. All are very still and quiet.*)

Simon . . . be nice to me, Simon. Be nice to me, dear Simon, and tell me.

SIMON. Dearest love, since I lost you—it was a long time ago. . . .

MARY ROSE (*petulant, and appealing*). It wasn't—please, it wasn't. (*She turns and moves to* MRS. MORLAND.) Tell me, Mother dear.

MORLAND. I don't know what she wants to be told.

MRS. MORLAND. I know.

MARY ROSE (*in a low voice, like an unhappy child*). Where is my baby ?

(*They cannot answer her. She looks at them all, then turns from* MRS. MORLAND *and runs up and off* L.C. SIMON *and* MRS. MORLAND *go swiftly after her.* MORLAND *and* CAMERON *are left alone. There is a pause. They are very conscious of what may be going on in that inner room.* CAMERON *sits in the chair* R. *of the table.* MORLAND *moves to* L. *of the table.*)

MORLAND. Have you been in this part of the country before, Mr. Cameron ?

CAMERON. No, sir. I haf not. It iss my first visit to England.

(*They are merely making talk—hardly hearing each other. Their minds are on the inner room.*)

Nefer, except in the railway train, haf I been so far from the sea. You cannot hear the sea in this place. It iss strange to me. (*His eyes stray to the door* L.C.)

MORLAND. We are twenty. miles or more from the sea, but our Downs are much admired. I hope you will give me the pleasure of showing them to you while you are here.

(CAMERON *forces his eyes away from the door.*)

CAMERON (*vaguely, but kind to the old man*). I thank you ferry much, Mr. Morland, but—in such circumstances do not trouble about me at all.

(*He rises, moves above the table, his eyes on the door* L.C. *They are both listening, but no sound comes from the inner room.*)

MORLAND. I am a print collector in a small way, I do not know if you are interested in prints. I have a pencil sketch by Cousins—undoubtedly genuine.

CAMERON (*moving to behind* MORLAND'S *chair*). I regret my

ignorance on the subject. This matter, so strange—so inexplicable——

MORLAND (*without emotion—he has no more capacity for it*). Please don't talk of it to me, sir. I am—an old man. I have been so occupied all my life with little things—very pleasant—I cannot cope—cannot cope——

(CAMERON *puts a sympathetic hand on his shoulder.* MORLAND *speaks in a quavering whisper.*)

Do you think she should have come back, Mr. Cameron ?

(CAMERON'S *head turns slowly to the door up* L.C. *as the lighting fades out and—*

The CURTAIN *Falls.*

SCENE 2

SCENE.—*We see again the dismantled room of Scene 1, Act I. All is as it was when the* CURTAIN *fell on that scene except that it is now darker. The fire, though red, has burned low. We see* HARRY *indistinctly, sitting, staring at the fire with wide-open unblinking eyes. The door up* L.C. *is still open.*

MRS. OTERY *comes in at the door* R. *carrying a lighted candle and a large breakfast cup and saucer.*

MRS. OTERY. Here's your tea, mister. Are you sitting in the dark ? I haven't been more than the ten minutes I promised you. I was——

(*She stops short, startled by his appearance. She holds the candle nearer him, which is the only light in the room except for the feeble fire. We now see his face more clearly and that he is staring into the fire, like one seeing things so strange that he is deprived of the power of motion. It is like an open-eyed trance, and the very antithesis of sleep.*)

What's the matter, mister ? Here's the tea, mister. I've brought you a cup of tea, I've just been the ten minutes.
HARRY (*rising*). Wait a mo. (*He looks about him, like one taking his bearings. Then he stares at the passage, then at her.*) Gimme the tea !

(*He takes the mug, and drinks eagerly.* MRS. OTERY *crosses* L., *and puts the candle on the broken mantelshelf.*)

That's better. Thank you, missus.

(MRS. OTERY *takes the mug and puts it on the mantelshelf.* HARRY *again stares from the passage to her. She realizes that he has had some queer experience.*)

MRS. OTERY. Have you seen anything ?

(HARRY *goes up to the door and retreats from it to* O., *above the packing case, looking at the door all the time.*)

HARRY. Come here !

(MRS. OTERY *comes to him, on his* L.)

(*In a rough way.*) See here, as I sat in that chair—I wasn't sleeping, mind you—it's no dream, but things of the far past connected with this old house, things I know naught of—they came crowding out of their holes and gathered round me, till I saw—I saw them all so clear. I don't know what to think, woman. Never mind that. (*He sits on a packing case.*) Now then—tell me about this—ghost.

MRS. OTERY (R. *of the armchair*). It's no concern of yours.

HARRY. Yes, it is some concern of mine ! The folk that used to live here—the Morlands——

MRS. OTERY. That was the name. I suppose you heard it in the village ?

HARRY. I've heard it all my days. It's the name I bear. I'm one of the family.

MRS. OTERY (*who has suspected it*). Ah !

HARRY. I suppose that's what made them come to me as I sat here. Tell me about them.

MRS. OTERY. It's little I know. They were gone before my time. The old man and his wife, they grew too frail to live alone —they're with friends in some other part of the country, if they're still alive.

HARRY. They're still alive. I'm going to see them. (*Harshly.*) It's not *them* I'm asking you about.

MRS. OTERY. They had a son-in-law, a sailor. The war has made a great man of him.

HARRY. I'm going to see him, too. He is my father. Hard I used to think him, but I know better now. Go on—there's the other one.

MRS. OTERY. That was all.

HARRY. There's one more.

MRS. OTERY. She's dead. I never saw her in life.

HARRY (*pause*). Where is she buried ?

MRS. OTERY. Down by the church.

HARRY. Is there a stone ?

MRS. OTERY. Yes.

HARRY. Does it say her age ?

MRS. OTERY. No.

HARRY. Is that holy spot well taken care of ?

MRS. OTERY. You can see for yourself.

HARRY. I will see for myself. And so it's her ghost that haunts this house ?

(MRS. OTERY *shivers but does not answer.* HARRY *pretends to be cynical again.*)

There's no such thing as ghosts.   And yet—(*he looks at the chair*) is it true about folk having had this house and left in a hurry ?

(MRS. OTERY *nods.*)

Because of a ghost—a thing that can't be ?   (*But he is not so sure.   He takes a hasty glance at the passage.*)

MRS. OTERY.   When I came in, your eyes were staring.   I thought you had seen her.

HARRY.   Have you ever seen her yourself ?

(MRS. OTERY *nods.*)

Where ?   In this room ?

(MRS. OTERY *looks towards the inner room.*)

Ah !   Has she ever been seen out of that room ?

MRS. OTERY.   All over the house—in every room and on the stairs.   (*She moves towards him, as if defying his incredulity.*) I tell you I've met her on the stairs and she drew back to let me pass and said "Good evening," too, timid-like, and at another time she has gone by me like a rush of wind.

HARRY.   What is she like ?

MRS. OTERY.   She looks just like you or me.   But for all that she's as light as air.   I've seen—things.

HARRY.   So !   She's harmless, it seems ?

MRS. OTERY.   There's some wouldn't say that.   Them that left in a hurry.   If she thought you were keeping it from her she would do you a mischief.

HARRY.   Keeping what from her ?

MRS. OTERY.   Whatever it is she prowls about this cold house searching for, searching, searching.   I don't know what it is.

HARRY (*grimly, though he is really moved*).   Maybe I could tell you.   I dare say I could even put her in the way of finding him.

MRS. OTERY.   Then I wish to God you would, and let her rest.

HARRY (*bitterly of himself*).   My old dear, there's worse things than not finding what you're looking for—there's finding them so different from what you had hoped.   (*Clinging to his cynicism.*) A ghost !   Oh, no—and yet and yet——   (*Rising.*)   See here, I am going into that room.

MRS. OTERY.   As you like.   I care not.

HARRY (*crossing to the door up* L.C.).   I'll break open the door.

MRS. OTERY.   No need ;   it's not locked ;   (*crossing to* R.) I deceived you about that.

HARRY (*whose eyes have followed her*).   Oh !   I tried it, and it

E

wouldn't open. And you think she's (*with a jerk of his head*) in there ?

MRS. OTERY. She may be.

(HARRY *shivers*.)

HARRY (*coming down to* C.). Leave me here now. I have a call to make.

MRS. OTERY (*knowing his purpose*). I dunno. You think you're in no danger, but——

HARRY. That's how it's to be, missus.

(MRS. OTERY *hesitates, then goes to the door* R., *checking as he speaks again.*)

Just ten minutes you were out of the room, did you say ?

MRS. OTERY. That was all.

(*She exits.*)

HARRY. God !

(*Though he has carried it off so far with bravado, the uncanniness of the situation has gripped him, and deeper than this is his pity for* MARY ROSE. *He turns up to the door, checks, and then crosses to the mantel for the candle and takes it up to the door* L.C., *and exits.*

This takes all the light from the room, which becomes quite dark. HARRY *is seen to hold up the candle as if peering into the inner room, but evidently he sees nothing. He re-enters the room, shielding the candle with his hand so that it casts no light in front of him until he takes his hand away. Then he, and we, see* MARY ROSE *standing at* R.C. *She looks as we saw her last except that she is paler. She is wearing what seem to be the same clothes, but the colour has gone out of them. The candle in his hand lights* HARRY'S *face, but she is in a blue-grey light with which that part of the room is suffused, and she is a vague figure. The effect is that he always is in light and she is in semi-darkness. There must be no attempt at theatrical effects. The room is now much darker than when* MRS. OTERY *was present. For the moment,* MARY ROSE *does not move, but when she does, her movements should be quite noiseless and thus in contrast to* HARRY'S.

HARRY *gets a shock when he sees her, but is very quiet. All the best of him is really brought to the surface by this meeting, and he is very anxious in his rough way to be kind. Throughout he accepts her as a ghost, and it will be largely owing to his doing so that we do it ourselves.*

She is a little afraid of him, and he is at first too taken aback to speak, though he holds his ground.   He is not afraid of her.   No one could be afraid of this wistful little ghost.)

MARY ROSE (*after peering into his face.   Remaining in one place, and always a childish ghost*).   Have you come to buy the house ?

HARRY (*who retains the candle—after a moment's hesitation as to how to answer an unearthly visitant*).   Not me.

MARY ROSE (*defending it*).   It's a very nice house—— (*Doubtfully.*)   Isn't it ?

HARRY.   It was a nice house once.

MARY ROSE (*pleased*).   Wasn't it ?   (*Suspiciously.*)   Did *you* know this house ?

HARRY (*who feels that anything might happen if he took his eyes off her*).   When I was a young shaver.

MARY ROSE.   Young !   Was it you who laughed ?

HARRY.   When was that ?

MARY ROSE (*puzzling*).   There was once someone who laughed in this house.   (*Wistfully.*)   Don't you think laughter is a very pretty sound ?

HARRY (*out of his depths*).   Is it ?   I dare say.   I never thought about it.

MARY ROSE.   You are quite old.

HARRY.   I'm getting on.

MARY ROSE (*confidentially, for the subject is of great importance to her*).   Would you mind telling me why every one is so old ? (*She is suddenly curious about him.*)   I don't know you, do I ?

HARRY.   I wonder. . . .   Take a look.

(MARY ROSE *glides towards him, to* C., *and looks childishly.   He holds up the candle to show his face better, but not hers.*)

You might have seen me in the old days—playing about—outside in the garden—or even inside.

(MARY ROSE *is a little disturbed, but doesn't know why.*)

MARY ROSE.   You—you are not Simon, are you ?

HARRY.   No.   My name is Harry.   (*He knows this may trouble her.*)

MARY ROSE (*instantly stiffening, and retreating a step*).   *I* don't think so.   I strongly object to your saying that.

HARRY.   I'm a queer sort of cove, and I would like to hear you call me Harry.

MARY ROSE.   I decline.   (*Courteously.*)   I regret, but I absolutely decline.   (*She has now some distrust of him.*)

HARRY.   No offence.   (*His great pity for her now shows in his face.*)

MARY ROSE (*noticing it*).   I think you are sorry for me.

HARRY (*with heart*).   I am that.

MARY ROSE (*childishly*). I am sorry for me, too.

HARRY (*moved*). If only there was something I—— (*He is wanting desperately to help her—he looks at the chair.*) I don't know about ghosts—not a thing—can they sit down ? Could you—— (*He wants to put her in the chair. He goes to the chair and turns it to face more to* R.)

MARY ROSE. That is *your* chair.

HARRY (*taken aback*). What do you mean by that ?

MARY ROSE. That is where *you* were sitting.

HARRY (*uncomfortable*). Were you in this room when I was sitting there ?

MARY ROSE (*glancing at the passage*). I came in to look at you and just stood behind.

(HARRY *shivers, and feels for his knife. Then, remembering, he crosses to the packing case where he had left it. It is gone.*)

HARRY. Where is my knife ? (*Turning to her.*) Were you standing behind the chair with my knife in your hand ?

(MARY ROSE *is sullenly silent. He moves up on her* R.)

Give me my knife.

(MARY ROSE *has it in her right hand. He takes it, puts it in his pocket, then crosses to the mantel and puts the candle down.*)

(*To* L.C. *below the armchair.*) What made you take it ?

MARY ROSE. I thought perhaps you were the one.

HARRY. The one ?

MARY ROSE. The one who stole him from me.

HARRY. I see ! Godsake ! In a sort of way I suppose I am.

MARY ROSE (*moving a little towards him*). Give him back to me.

HARRY. I wish I could. But I'm doubting he is gone beyond recall.

MARY ROSE (*unexpectedly*). Who is he ?

HARRY (*surprised*). Do you mean you have forgotten whom you are searching for ?

MARY ROSE (*she nods*). I knew once. I can't remember. It is such a long time ago. I am so tired. (*Another pace towards him.*) Please can I go away and play now ?

HARRY. Go away ? Where ? You mean back to that—that place ?

(MARY ROSE *nods.*)

What sort of a place is it ? Do they play there ? Is it good to be there ?

MARY ROSE. Oh ! Lovely, lovely, lovely !

HARRY. It's not just the island, is it—that's so lovely ?

MARY ROSE. No.

HARRY. Is the island just the beginning of the loveliness ?
MARY ROSE. Yes !
HARRY. I thought that. Are they ghosts at that place ?
MARY ROSE (*surprised and emphatic*). No !
HARRY. You're sure ?
MARY ROSE. Honest Injun.
HARRY. · Are they—the dead ?
MARY ROSE. What is that ?
HARRY. It's near like as if some bit of Heaven had fallen down splash into that loch.
MARY ROSE (*cajoling, taking a further step to him*). Please, I don't want to be a ghost any more.
HARRY. It's no use your expecting me to be able to help you out of that. I'm at my wits' end. (*He sits in the armchair, and hesitates a moment.*) Ghostie, come to me. I wish you would.

(*He indicates that he wants, in a tender way, to take her on his knee.*)

. MARY ROSE (*understanding*). Certainly not.
HARRY. No ? If you'll come I'll try to help you.

(MARY ROSE *goes and sits on his knee without assistance from him.*)

Well, well ! See here, when I was sitting by the fire alone I seemed to hear you as you once were saying that some day when he was a man you would like to sit on your Harry's knee.
MARY ROSE (*quoting herself—but without expression*). The loveliest time of all will be when he is a man and takes me on his knee instead of my taking him on mine.

(*The fire and candle now light him, but not her and she is still unsubstantial-looking.*)

HARRY. Do you see who I am now ?
MARY ROSE. Nice man.
HARRY. Is that all you know about me ?
MARY ROSE. ˙ Yes.
HARRY. There's a name I'd like to call you by, but best not to worry you—poor Ghostie. (*He is helpless.*) I wonder if there was ever a man with a ghost on his knee before.
MARY ROSE (*innocently*). I don't know.
HARRY. Seems to me you're feared of being a ghost.
MARY ROSE. Yes.
HARRY. I dare say, to a timid soul, being a ghost is worse than seeing them.
MARY ROSE. Yes.
HARRY. Is it lonely being a ghost ?
MARY ROSE. Yes.
HARRY. Do you know any other ghosts ?
MARY ROSE (*sadly*). No.

HARRY. Would you like to know other ghosts ?

MARY ROSE. Yes.

HARRY. I can understand that. And now you would like to go away and play ?

MARY ROSE. Please.

HARRY. In this cold house, when you should be searching, do you sometimes play by yourself instead ?

MARY ROSE. Yes. Don't tell !

HARRY. Not me ! You're a pretty thing. (*As to a child.*) What beautiful shoes you have.

(MARY ROSE *holds out her feet complacently.*)

MARY ROSE. Nice buckles.

HARRY. I like your hair.

MARY ROSE. Pretty hair.

HARRY. Do you mind the tuft that used to stand up at the back of—of Simon's head ?

MARY ROSE (*merrily*). Naughty tuft !

HARRY. I have one like that. (*He takes off his hat and the tuft shows.*)

MARY ROSE. Oh dear, oh dear, what a naughty tuft.

(*She seems to smooth it down, but being a ghost, she doesn't really touch it—nor is his arm round her though she is on his knee.*)

HARRY. My name's Harry.

MARY ROSE (*happily, but without much meaning*). Harry, Harry, Harry, Harry !

(*They have been quite gay for the moment.*)

HARRY. But you don't know what Harry I am.

MARY ROSE. No.

HARRY. But this brings us no nearer to what's to be done with you. They say there's ways of laying ghosts, but I'm so ignorant.

MARY ROSE. Tell me !

HARRY. I wish I could ; you're even more ignorant than I am.

MARY ROSE. Tell me.

HARRY. All I know about them for certain is that they are unhappy because they can't find something, and then once they've got the thing they want, they go away happy and never come back.

MARY ROSE. Oh, nice ! (*Her head has dropped as with fatigue.*)

HARRY. But where do they go to, that's what does us. You've got the thing you want at last and you're dog-tired. What you need now is to get back to that place you say is lovely.

. . .

MARY ROSE. Yes! Yes!

HARRY. You know it's lovely, but you can say no more about it.

MARY ROSE. No.

HARRY. Queer—you that know so much can tell nothing, and them that know nothing can tell so much. If there was any way of getting you to that place.

MARY ROSE. Tell me!

HARRY (*desperate*). They would surely come for you, if they wanted you.

MARY ROSE (*frightened by the soundness of the argument*). Yes.

HARRY (*who is entirely honest*). It's like as if they had forgot you.

MARY ROSE (*in distress*). Yes.

HARRY. It's as if nobody wanted you—nobody needed you.

MARY ROSE. Yes. (*She gets off his knee and moves* C.) Bad man!

HARRY (*wryly*). It's easy to call me names, but how should the likes of me know what to do with a ghost who has lost her way on earth; a mere man's so helpless—so helpless.

(*Cue : The organ-pipe is heard, followed by the Call of the Island.*)

(*He sees that a change is coming over her.*)   What is it? Do you hear anything? There isn't a sound.

(*Though he hears nothing the Call of the Island begins to be heard by* MARY ROSE *and us when he said " so helpless " and continues to the end of the play. The organ-pipe is the only effect used in this act. The windows open automatically during the " Call."*
At first we only see her vaguely in the distance standing there, but gradually a heavenly light is cast upon her face, and we see her arms going out in an ecstasy of joy. The great glory is coming to her. In the music are sweet voices calling—" Mary Rose! Mary Rose! " She slowly turns with arms still outstretched till she is facing the window. Now a shooting star shoots down—(the organ-pipe ceases) as if it were her star come for her and then—still with arms out—she walks out at the window—straight out—trustingly into the Empyrean. The music comes to an end. HARRY has been staring at her, but is not much seen in the darkness, for it is only she who is in the pool of light. He goes to the window and stares out.)

CURTAIN.

PROPERTY PLOT

ACT I, Scene 1

1 old stuffed armchair.
1 large packing case with cork top.
1 small ditto.
1 black paint can on mantel-board.
Sacking at window.

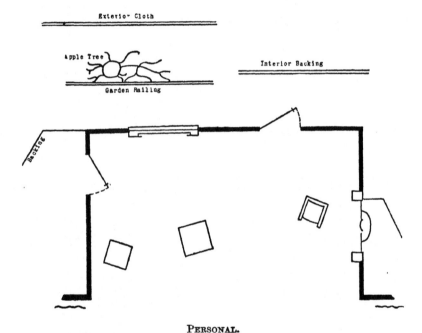

PERSONAL.

Trench knife in case ⎫
Dummy cake of tobacco ⎬ (for HARRY).
Pipe ⎭
Box of matches

ACT I, Scene 2

1. Aubusson carpet.
2. Cabriole leg table.
   On it.—3 well-bound books.
      10 various engravings.
   On floor R. of it.—A " Gainsborough " drawing between two white
      cardboards.
3. Small stuffed easy chair.
4. High-backed winged armchair.
5. Ribbon-backed Chippendale armchair.
6. Ribbon-backed Chippendale ordinary chair.

7. Early Victorian footstool.
8. Fire screen with peacock tapestry panel on tripod legs.
9. Queen Anne bureau.

> *On it.*—2 small black bronze vases.
> Black bronze flower stand containing poppies.
>
> *In right-hand drawer.*—A " Turner " drawing.

10. Queen Anne chest on stand.

> *On it.*—A clock with the working figure of a smith striking an anvil.
> 2 brass candlesticks.

11. Brass fender and set of brasses.
12. Chesterfield settee.

> *On it.*—Copy of " The Times," 1880.
> 2 soft cushions.
> Knitting and needles for MRS. MORLAND.

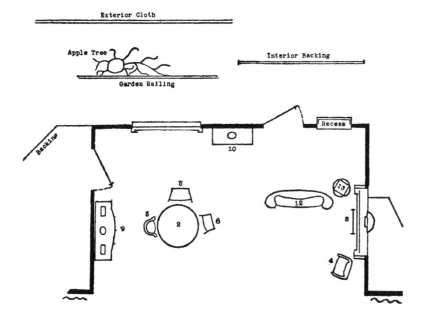

13. Small occasional table with pie-crust top.

> *On it.*—Work-basket.
> 3 books.
> Paper knife.

14. Brass log box.
    Mantelpiece.

> *On it.*—4 Chelsea figures.
> 3 papier-maché vases.
>
> *Over it.*—Painted oil colour in gilt frame.

In built Recess up L.—On shelf, 3 papier-maché vases.
On base, 1 large green papier-maché vase containing apple blossom.
2 ditto blue vases.
2 ditto coloured vases.

In recessed Bookcase.—3 sets of bound books.

   On shelf at top.—2 blue china cups and saucers.
      2 blue china plates.
      1 green vase.
7 oval head and shoulder crayons in gilt frames in small panels.
1 pair of pink flowered linen curtains to window.
Stone hearth 4 inches high, quite bare and clean in this scene.

NOTE.—The coverings for this scene on the settee, armchairs, chair
      bottoms, footstool and cushions should be of a soft pink flowered
      linen, very delicate and toning in with the apple blossom.

      The curtains are made of the same material and hang straight down
      reaching to the floor.

An apple tree in full blossom comes over the stone balustrade at the back
and one arm of it goes right across the balcony from R. to L.
PROPS. OFF STAGE.—Fishing rod (2 lengths) and reel.
   Clock chimes.
PERSONAL PROPS.—Pocket magnifying glasses for AMY and MORLAND.

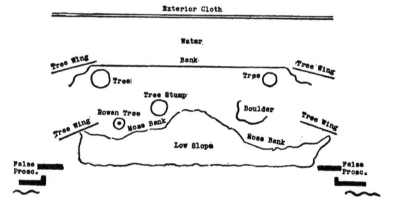

ACT II

2 boat runner grooves.
Small fishing boat on truck, 6 ft. long by 3 ft. 6 in. beam.
Small stunted rowan tree, 5 ft. high covered with clusters of red berries.
Bundle of loose twigs for SIMON to make up fire.
4 property stones to look wet.
Tree-stump sticking up 3 ft. above the platform, covered with loose moss.
   Underneath the moss is carved letters M A R.
Pieces of grass matting.
Small stump for tying boat up to.
Loose twigs and branches to dress sides of stage.
6 rock pieces.
2 lines to pull boat on and off.

In Boat.—Painter.
   2 wet-looking oars.
   Pair of wood rowlocks.
   Fishing rod in two pieces.
   A landing net.
   2 property trout.
   2 pieces of newspaper, varnished to look wet.
   Fishing creel.

In it.—2 bottles ginger ale, dummy.
1 pot of pickles.
1 pot of marmalade, plates, knives, forks, 2 of each.
2 apples in paper bag.
Small table cloth.
2 serviettes.
Sponge cake sandwich in paper for CAMERON's "butcher meat."
Off Stage.—2 property trout filled with sponge cake wrapped in burnt paper out of sight by fire R.
EFFECTS.—64-foot organ-pipe stopped and bellows.
Wind machine.
Rain barrel.
PERSONAL PROPERTIES.—Pipe⎫
Pouch   ⎬for SIMON.
Box of safety matches   ⎭
Small bound book, "Euripides," for CAMERON.

ACT III, SCENE 1

Same as Act I, Scene 2, excepting :
The coverings used in that scene are now removed from the furniture.
The pink curtains are replaced by blue ones to match the furniture, and are on a rod and are practical.
The apple tree is now in fruit.
The window is closed.

1. *Queen Anne bureau* R.
   Black bronze flower stand on it now contain carnations.
   There is now a telephone on it.

2. *Cabriole leg table* R.C.
   On it.—"Tatler."
   3 newspapers.
   3 books.
   1 large book of engravings.

3. *Chesterfield settee* L.C.
   On it.—Book.
   "Punch."
   Large reading-glass.

4. *Small occasional table* L.C.
   On it.—3 books.
   1 large box of matches.
   Crochet work and needle.
   Duplicate telegram in work-basket.

In built Recess up L.—Large green vase replaced by large black one containing chrysanthemums.
The fire screen now covered with black gauze to give it a faded look is up L., across corner of room.
At Table R.C.—Chair 5 replaces chair 6.
Chair 3 replaces chair 5.
Chair 6 replaces chair 3.
Down Stage L.—Chair 4 is now turned to half-face audience.
Off Stage (in room up L.).—Telegram in envelope.

ACT III, SCENE 2

Same as Act I, Scene 1.
Additional :
   Off R.—Large teacup   ⎫
      Candlestick (candle alight)⎬for MRS. OTERY.
   Knife for MARY ROSE.

LIGHTING PLOT

Floats and Nos. 1, 2, 3 and 4 Battens {1 white and amber circuit
1 small white circuit.
1 blue circuit.

Floats and battens are divided up into 4 sections each, in each circuit, numbering Number 1 section from L. to R. 4 baby spots under No. 1 batten numbered as follows from L. to R.:

No. 1. Blue No. 18. Set to cover armchair 2nd position in last scene

No. 2. Blue No. 18. Set to cover MARY ROSE when sitting on SIMON'S knee in last scene.

No. 3. Blue No. 18. Set to produce MARY ROSE R.C. as "ghost."

No. 4. White. Set to cover MARY ROSE R.C. during "Call."

Note : If a spot batten is not available, the above lighting from perches.

ACT I, *Scene* 1.—Twig fire with heater for smoke and lamps to grow up from nothing.

½-watt focus lamp. Fire amber used with it.

ACT II.—Camp twig fire with heater for smoke and lamps to grow up from nothing.

ACT III, *Scene* 1.—Log fire and ½-watt focus lamp used with it.

2 two-light Louis candle brackets.

2 three-light Louis candle brackets.

Note : The lights during the play will always creep up or down and never be hurried, so that one hardly notices a change in the light while it is going on. This is especially necessary in the first scene and last scene of the play to help the weird effect.

LIGHTS IN FRONT OF HOUSE

The orchestra should be entirely screened in.

Before the Prelude of each act the house lights should be slowly lowered and then, and not till then, should the music of the Prelude start.

During the scene changes in Acts I and III, the house lights should be kept lowered.

LIGHTING PLOT

ACT I

SCENE 1

To Open.—*As the* CURTAIN *rises.*—Blue float (Sections 2 and 3) FULL UP. White and amber length outside window.

Cue 1.—*When the* CURTAIN *is up.*—Creep up Sections 2 and 3 white, and amber lengths up to ¾.

Cue 2.—*As* HARRY *pulls down the sacking from the window.*—Extra circuit white floats (Sections 2 and 3) creep up to ½ ; white and amber floats (Sections 2 and 3) creep up to full.

Cue 2A.—*As* HARRY *lights the fire.*—Fire (*with smoke effect*) not alight at opening, comes up slowly flickering to a red-amber flow. A ½-watt focus lamp in fire comes up with it.

Cue 3.—MRS. OTERY. " It's so far from a town."—Take out slowly white circuit of float and check blue float to ¾ : window length and white and amber float to ¼.

Cue 4.—HARRY, *left alone at the end of the scene, sits in the chair, looks at* C., *then, at the door up* L.C.—Take out slowly white and amber and blue floats. Fire slowly fades out last.

BLACK OUT.

76

SCENE 2

Opening dark. *To Open.*—Black out.

Cue 5.—*When the* CURTAIN *is up, as the Prelude ends.*—Blue baby spot
No. 3 slowly up to $\frac{1}{3}$ so that the figures at table are just visible.
Followed by : All coming up slowly together to FULL UP.

Float.—White and amber circuit.
White circuit.
No. 1 Batten.—White and amber circuit.
No. 4 Batten.—3 and 4 Sections white and amber circuit.
Perches.—L., 1 $\frac{1}{2}$-watt (light amber) on table R.
   R., 1 $\frac{1}{2}$-watt (light amber) on settee L.
   1 $\frac{1}{2}$-watt (light amber) in alcove L.
Lengths.—1 white and amber above window.
   1 white and amber behind balustrade.
   1 white and amber L. of window.
   1 small (4 lamps) white and amber to inner bedroom L.C.
   1 small (4 lamps) white and amber to door R.

Take out spot No. 3 when FULL UP.
No fire. Hearth empty.

No change of light during Scene.

ACT II

To Open.—Black out.

CURTAIN RISE.

Cue 6.—*As the Prelude ends.*—Slowly come up together to FULL. Blue
circuit slightly in front.
Float.—White and amber circuit.
   White circuit.
   Blue circuit.
Batten.—Nos. 2, 3 and 4.
   Ditto.
Lengths.—2 long blue behind water row.
Perches.—L., 1 $\frac{1}{2}$-watt light amber on tree stump.
   1 $\frac{1}{2}$-watt light amber on fir tree.
   R., 1 $\frac{1}{2}$-watt light amber on tree stump.
   1 $\frac{1}{2}$-watt light amber on R.C. down stage.
When all FULL UP by last bar of music take out blue float and battens.

Cue 6A.—*As* SIMON *puts a match to the fire.*—Smoke rises from heater and
fire comes in.

Cue 7.—*On the second entrance of* CAMERON *in the boat.*—Bring in blue float
and batten with the addition of No. 1 blue batten and No. 2 blue baby
spot. (As SIMON stamps out fire take fire lamps off).

Cue 8.—*As* SIMON *exits for the second time.*—All amber and white float and
batten slowly out, leaving all blue and baby spot.

ACT III

SCENE 1

4 Louis Candle Brackets with yellow shades have now been installed
in the room with a switch below door on wall R. The position of these are :
2 three-light brackets. 1 R. of window. 1 L. of L.C. door.
2 two-light brackets. 1 each side of fire breast.

To Open.—*Floats.*—White and amber circuit FULL UP.
   White circuit FULL UP.

No. 1 Batten.—Nos. 2 and 3 Sections white and amber FULL UP.
 Nos. 2 and 3 Sections white circuit FULL UP.
Lengths.—To window. Large white and amber FULL UP.
 Door up L.C. Small amber length (4 lamps).
 Door R. Small amber length (4 lamps).
Perches.—1 amber ½-watt from L. on table R.
Log Fire L.—Burning brightly.
 Fire amber ½-watt through fireplace on to settee, *Working.*

Cue 9.—*After* AMY's *final exit.*—Check bunch light at window slowly.
 Check white float to ½.
 Remaining float and batten to ¾.

Cue 10.—*As* MORLAND *switches on the lights.*—Brackets light up.
 Floats and battens back to FULL.
 Take everything exterior to the room out.

Cue 11.—CAMERON. " You cannot hear the sea in this place . . ."—
 Bring No. 3 baby spot in.

Cue 12.—MORLAND. " Do you think she should have come back, Mr.
 Cameron ? "—Everything slowly fades out. No. 3 baby spot
 being last away.

BLACK OUT.

SCENE 2

To Open.—Black out.

Cue 13.—CURTAIN *up.* End of Prelude.—Twig fire and ½-watt fire lamp
 slowly up.
 Nos. 2 and 3 Sections blue float slowly up to ½.

Cue 14.—To follow Cue No. 13.—Nos. 2 and 3 Sections white and amber
 float come up to ½.

Cue 14A.—HARRY. " Wait a mo." (*He looks about him—bus.*).—Same
 sections up to ¾.

Cue 14B.—HARRY. " I have a call to make."—Fire slowly dies out.

Cue 15.—HARRY *exits into the passage with candle.*—Float out.

Cue 16.—HARRY *returns from the passage with the candle.* MARY ROSE *in
 position* R.C.—Baby spot No. 3 slowly in. MARY ROSE should come
 visible to the audience at the same time as HARRY sees her. Fire
 slowly comes in again.

Cue 16A.—HARRY. " . . . Take a look." (*As* MARY ROSE *glides towards
 him to* C.)—Bring in baby spot No. 2 half up very slowly, followed by
 No. 1.

Cue 17.—*As* MARY ROSE *moves to the armchair to sit on* HARRY's *knee.*—
 Check out baby spot No. 3. Nos. 1 and 2 come up to FULL.
 The ½-watt focus fire lamp should be so placed that it strikes HARRY's,
 face full but not MARY ROSE when she is sitting on his knees.

Cue 18.—HARRY. " It's easy to call me names . . ."—Take out baby
 spots Nos. 1 and 2 and bring in No. 3 only half up, and slowly take
 fire light off.

Cue 18A.—HARRY. " . . . so helpless . . . helpless . . ." (*As the organ
 pipe comes in.*)—2 ½-watt focus lamps on star cloth come on from
 back.

Cue 19.—MARY ROSE *raises her arms.*—Bring in baby spot No. 4 to FULL
 and No. 3 to FULL.

Cue 20.—*As* MARY ROSE *turns up stage and faces the window.*—Baby spot
 No. 4 goes out leaving No. 3 only.

Cue 20A.—MARY ROSE *turns and fully faces the window.* (*Singing off :* " Mary Rose ! Mary Rose !)—A shooting star effect, star going from left to right is seen.

Cue 21.—*As* MARY ROSE *begins to move up stage.*—No. 3 baby spot slowly goes out.

The only light left on the stage is now the candle which is masked from the window as it is on the mantel-board and this ends the Scene.

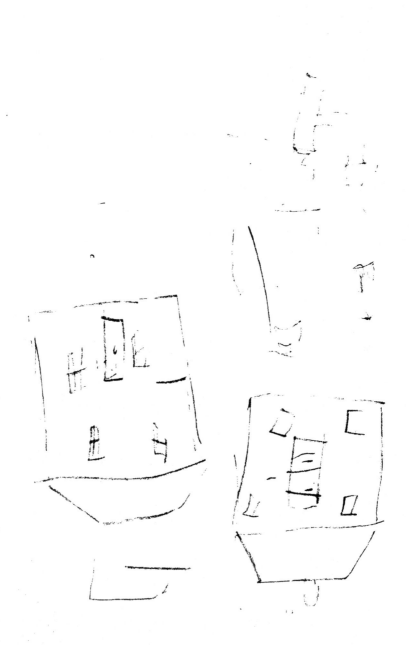